A NATURALIST'S GUIDE TO ST. SIMONS ISLAND

Written by
H. E. TAYLOR SCHOETTLE

Illustrated by
JENNIFER SMITH

D1131419

Layout by
TAYLOR SCHOETTLE

Computer Graphics & Typesetting by
TOMMY JENKINS

Produced by
WATERMARKS PRINTING COMPANY
St. Simons Island, GA

Printed by
THE DARIEN NEWS, INC.
Darien , GA

Library of Congress Catalog Card Number: 93-61513

ACKNOWLEDGMENTS

I would like to thank the following for their helpful comments and suggestions on the content of this work: William Way, James Gould, Jack Conyers, and Mary Gash, who have devoted interests in this area and have lived a great part of their lives on St. Simons Island; Will Hon, a naturalist and artist, employed as a Marine Education Specialist for the University of Georgia Marine Extension Service at Skidaway Island, Savannah; and my oldest son, Christopher Schoettle. I would like to recognize Kay Jenkins, Jim Pettigrew, Jr. and Mary Gash for their editorial work on the manuscript.

I would like to thank my wife, Marie Schoettle, whose steady hand made the final ink renderings of the maps and diagrams in the Figures. Figures 2, 4, 7, 8, 10, 11, 12, 15, and 25 have been modified from the work of Charlotte Ingram and Carol Johnson in the Field Guide to Jekyll Island, with the permission of its publisher, The University of Georgia. The plant and animal drawings in Appendix A and B that are not initialed were also transferred from the Jekyll Island field guide. These were done by Carol Johnson.

The illustration of the owl on the signpost, Site 15, and the heron flying over the marsh, in the Introduction, are drawings by Laurel McCook.

The drawing of Christ Church, in the History section, was modified from a photograph taken by Dorothy Paulk McClain.

The depiction of the Georgia Martyrs, in the History section, is a drawing of the sculpture by Marjorie Lawrence.

CONTENTS

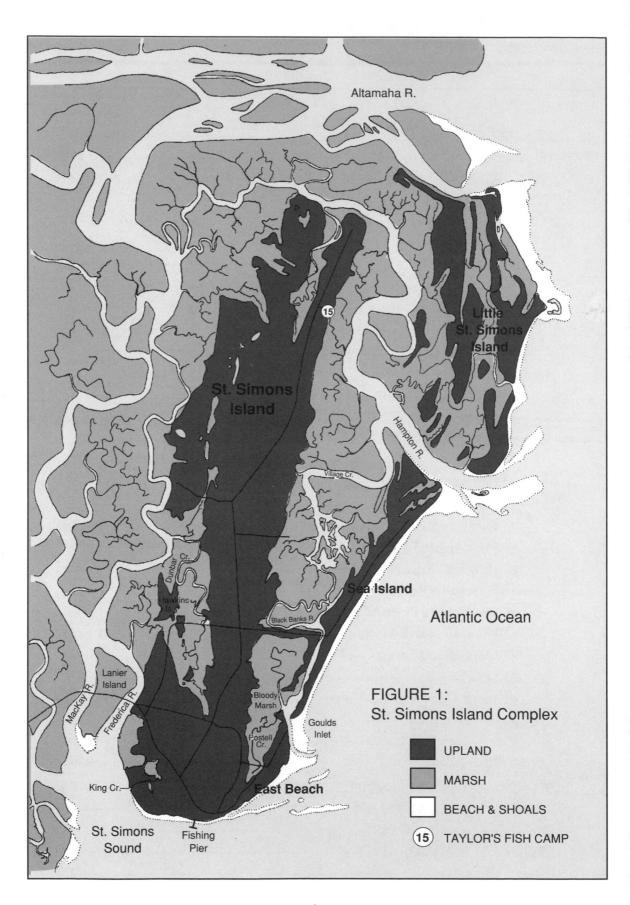

Altamaha R.

Little
St. Simons
Island

St. Simons
Island

Hampton R.

Village Cr.

Sea Island

Atlantic Ocean

Dunbar Cr.

Hawkins Is.

Black Banks R.

Lanier
Island

MacKay R.

Frederica R.

Bloody
Marsh

Goulds
Inlet

Postell
Cr.

King Cr.

East Beach

St. Simons
Sound

Fishing
Pier

FIGURE 1:
St. Simons Island Complex

■ UPLAND

▨ MARSH

□ BEACH & SHOALS

⑮ TAYLOR'S FISH CAMP

PREFACE

This guide is divided into three sections. The first describes the physical setting, geology and ecological environments of the barrier islands of Georgia. Here, a general view of the geological history and physical forces that create the characteristic shapes and dynamic changes of the Georgia barrier islands is disclosed. The ecological features that characterize the ocean beaches, salt marshes, maritime forests and freshwater sloughs are described and diagrammed. You are encouraged to read this section before visiting the sites.

The second section presents the sites to be visited on St. Simons Island. The sites not only describe each of the designated areas of St. Simons, but often provide examples of the general phenomena described in the first section. Cross-references connecting related information between these two sections frequently occur throughout both texts.

Appendix A is a guide to the identification of the common plants found in the various ecological settings of St. Simons Island. Appendix B identifies the living animals most frequently found on St. Simons' beaches and marshes. Appendix C is a list of recommended books and field guides. Appendix D is a bibliography.

This publication is intended for anyone interested in learning more about the natural history of Georgia's barrier islands. It is hoped that educators will find this guide to be an avenue to incorporate the coast of Georgia into their curricula. By being better informed on the nature and dynamics of barrier islands, we and future generations will be able to make better decisions on maintaining a healthy coastal environment and preserving these serenely beautiful islands.

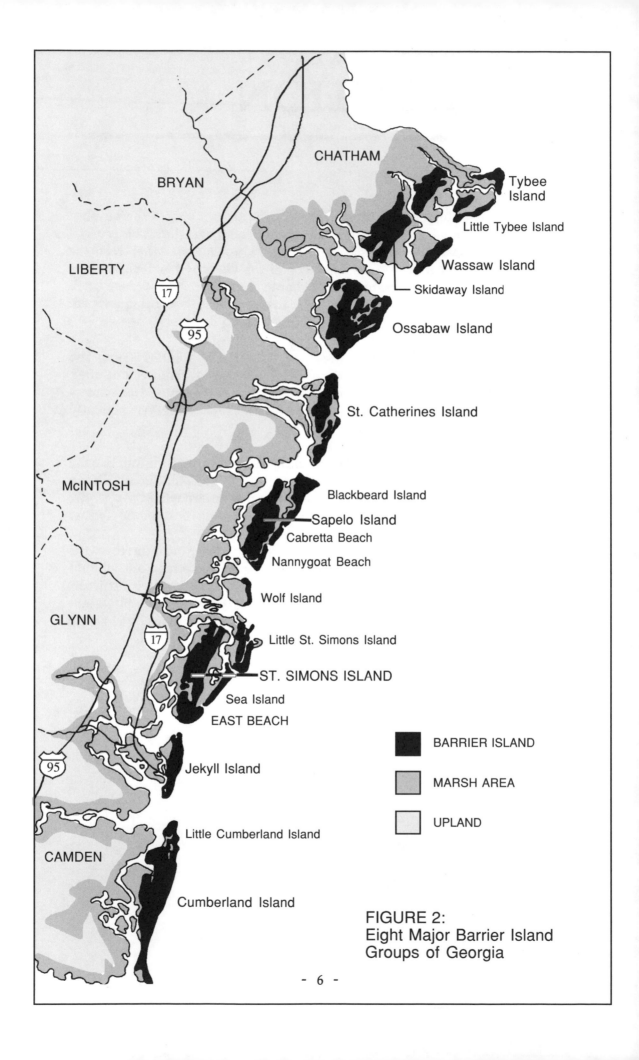

CHATHAM

BRYAN

Tybee Island

Little Tybee Island

Wassaw Island

LIBERTY

Skidaway Island

17

95

Ossabaw Island

St. Catherines Island

McINTOSH

Blackbeard Island

Sapelo Island

Cabretta Beach

Nannygoat Beach

Wolf Island

GLYNN

Little St. Simons Island

17

ST. SIMONS ISLAND

Sea Island

EAST BEACH

95

Jekyll Island

Little Cumberland Island

CAMDEN

Cumberland Island

BARRIER ISLAND

MARSH AREA

UPLAND

FIGURE 2:
Eight Major Barrier Island
Groups of Georgia

INTRODUCTION

Along the coast of Georgia, eight clusters of barrier islands are separated from the mainland by an extensive system of salt marshes and sounds (see Figure 2). Barrier islands form most of the beaches of the Atlantic and Gulf states. The barrier beaches receive the full brunt of oceanic storms and the salt marshes absorb much of the wave and storm energy that gets around or comes over the barrier islands; hence, the term barrier.

Unlike many of the developed barrier islands of the east coast, the Georgia barrier islands still retain much of their native wilderness. Approximately two-thirds of the islands are in wild states. Most of these are designated as parks, wildlife refuges, research sites and heritage preserves, with limited access or they are inaccessible.

The four barrier islands accessible by causeway are Jekyll Island, St. Simons Island, Sea Island and Tybee Island. They differ from each other in their degree of development and the type of communities they contain. Jekyll Island is a state park with limited housing and with much of its area preserved in a natural state. For this reason, Jekyll Island was chosen to be the subject of my first field guide, published in 1983.[6] Jekyll has a small resident population and a large tourist trade. Sea Island is privately owned by the Sea Island Company. It has one hotel and condominiums which serve tourists and seasonal guests, but a large part of the island is occupied by Sea Island residents. Tybee Island is a small, residential island which is utilized by many day visitors from the greater Savannah area and has a moderate tourist trade. St. Simons Island is also primarily residential with a rising trend in tourism. Due to the island's large size, population growth and development continue to rise.

St. Simons has had a long and complex history of human occupancy which, combined with its many natural features, makes the island a fascinating place to explore from a naturalist's point of view.

Taylor Schoettle
P.O. Box 1117
Darien, Georgia 31305

PHYSICAL SETTING

St. Simons Island, Sea Island, and Little St. Simons Island are a complex of three barrier islands located north of Jekyll Island and south of Sapelo Island (see Figures 1 and 2). St. Simons Island is an older (Pleistocene) island, 11 1/2 miles long, and from 1/2 to 2 1/2 miles wide. Its 31-square mile area makes St. Simons second to Cumberland as largest of Georgia's barrier islands. Included in this study is the younger (Holocene) island of East Beach which is now attached to St. Simons Island at its southern end. East Beach is about 1 1/2 miles long and approximately 1/2 of a mile wide at its most expanded point. (The terms Holocene and Pleistocene are explained in the Geology section).

CLIMATE AND WEATHER

The climate of this coastal region is moderate, with short winters and long springs and falls. Temperatures during the warmest months (July and August) range from the 80s to the high 90s. From December to March, temperatures usually range from the high 40s to the low 70s, with occasional freezes. Because of the moderating effects of the ocean and sea breezes, temperatures on barrier islands are less extreme than those on the coastal mainland.

Average annual rainfall on the coastal islands ranges from 30 to 50 inches. During the summer months, a large high-pressure system called the "Bermuda High" settles in this area and is responsible for diverting most large continental storms away from this area of the Southeast. Therefore, most summer rains come from local afternoon thundershowers. On a typical summer day, the air over the pine-covered mainland heats up and rises. These upward-moving air currents (convections) pull moisture-laden air in from the oceans, creating the sea breezes which get stronger as the day progresses. In the colder upper strata high above the pine lands, moisture in the air condenses to form clouds. Towards the afternoon, great thunderheads form in the west and migrate shoreward, often bringing short-lived squalls with pelting rain -- a brief respite for a sun-baked land. In the evenings, the earth cools quickly, disrupting the convection currents over the land. Because water retains heat, the air over the water now rises a little faster than that over the cooler mainland, which creates gentle land breezes during the night. (See Figure 3.)

Glassy-calm mornings are typical as the land warms, temporarily equaling the temperature of the water. As the land gradually heats up, the land convections again usher forth the day's sea breezes. Summer droughts, which have become more frequent in the past decade, occur when these convection currents fail to produce rains for extended periods of time.

In late summer, the Bermuda High disintegrates, allowing the coast to again receive rain from large frontal storm systems which move across the continental United States. In the fall tropical storms can bring the heaviest rainfalls. Intermittent northeasters, which may last for several days at a time, supply most of the rain in the late fall, winter, and spring.

Prevailing winds are from the west and southeast in summer and from the north and northeast in winter. The strongest winds are usually out of the northeast. Hurricanes pass over or near the Georgia coast about once every ten years. Hurricanes tend to follow the path of warm air above the Gulf Stream near the edge of the continental shelf, about 80 miles off our coast. Looking at Figure 4, one can appreciate how the extreme westward position of this area often places it out of the path of hurricanes coming up the Atlantic coast.

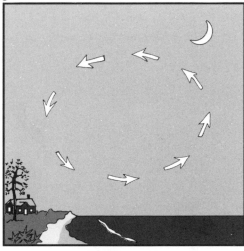

Day (Sea Breezes)   Night (Land Breezes)

FIGURE 3: Daily Cycle of Wind Circulation
(Modified from Fox, 1983)[1]

TIDES AND WAVES

Typical of tidal patterns along the southeastern coast, Georgia has two high tides and two low tides each day. The range of Georgia tides, however, is not typical. While Cape Hatteras, to the north, has 2- to 3-foot tides and Miami, to the south, has 1- to 2-foot tides, the Georgia coast has 6.5- to 9-foot tides.

Figure 4 shows that the coast of Georgia is the most westward location of the Atlantic seaboard of the United States. It is in the approximate center of the inward-curving coastline known as the South Atlantic Bight, which extends from Cape Hatteras, North Carolina, to Miami, Florida. The offshore tidal range of the Atlantic Ocean is approximately 2 to 3 feet. Since the incoming tide reaches Cape Hatteras and Miami first, these areas receive tidal ranges that closely reflect those of the open ocean. As the water funnels into the Bight, it piles up on itself, creating a graded increase of the tidal ranges toward the middle of the Bight. Since St. Simons and Jekyll Islands are at the inward-most point of the Bight, they receive the highest tidal range. The high tides and extremely gradual slope of Georgia's coastal plain allow tidal waters to penetrate deeply into the land, creating the most expansive marshes of the entire Atlantic coast.

Except under storm conditions, wave energy on the coast of Georgia is low. The energy of the large waves coming from the open ocean is dissipated by bottom friction as the waves move across the broad, shallow waters over the continental shelf. Offshore sandbars and inlet shoals effect further loss of wave energy by causing the waves to break over them before reaching the beaches. (The Geology section describes the nature of the continental shelf and its shoals).

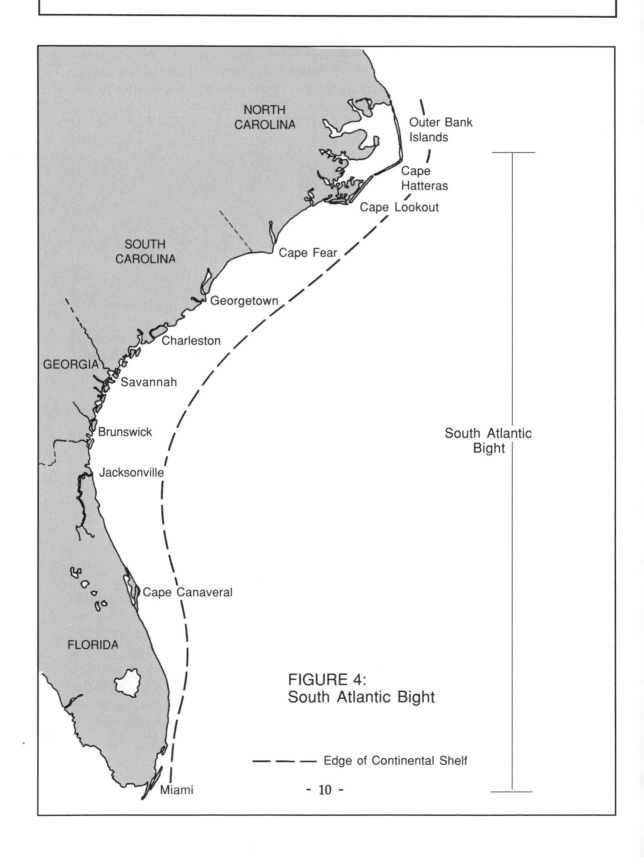

FIGURE 4:
South Atlantic Bight

— — — Edge of Continental Shelf

GEOLOGY

GEOLOGICAL HISTORY AND POSITIONING OF BARRIER ISLANDS

Figure 5 shows the three major topographic regions of Georgia. The coastal plain was ocean bottom as recently as 40 million years ago during the Oligocene Epoch and the fall line was the shore of that ancient ocean.[2] Today the coastal plain is mostly flat pine lands which cover the southeastern half of the state.

The continental shelf is the remaining submerged portion of the coastal plain. Glynn County's extreme westward position places its shore further away from the outer edge of the continental shelf (continental slope) than the other shorelines of the South Atlantic Bight. This places Glynn County's beaches about 80 miles from the continental slope (see Figure 4). From Georgia's coast, the continental shelf declines very gradually, averaging 1 to 2 feet per mile. The continental slope is the actual edge of the continent whose slope rapidly falls to a deep plateau and eventually into the ocean depths, two miles down.

FIGURE 5:
Topographic Regions of Georgia

Over the past million or so years, the Pleistocene Epoch to present, climatic changes have caused Georgia's shoreline to vacillate from the continental slope to 60 miles inland from our present shoreline. Seven sets of barrier island profiles have been identified over the 60-mile inland stretch (see Figure 6). The oldest and largest of these relic barrier islands is Trail Ridge in the Wicomico Island sequence. Its great size and position indicate that the island did much to obstruct the drainage of the flat lands to its west when the sea level declined close to a million years ago. This obstruction contributed to the formation of the 700-square mile Okefenokee Swamp (see Figure 5), and diverted rivers on its western border to the Gulf of Mexico. The focus of this guide, however, is directed to the two sets of barrier islands closest to the ocean.

Georgia's present-day barrier islands are actually a mid-portion of a system of sandy barriers which extend from the middle of the South Carolina coast to the

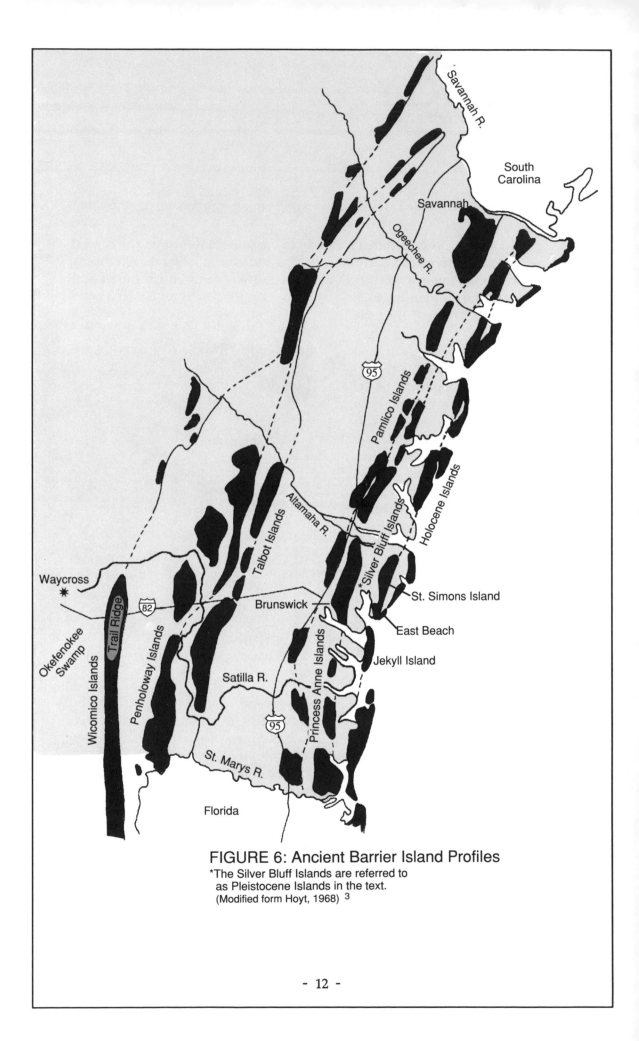

FIGURE 6: Ancient Barrier Island Profiles

*The Silver Bluff Islands are referred to
as Pleistocene Islands in the text.
(Modified form Hoyt, 1968) [3]

mouth of the St. Johns River in Jacksonville, Florida (see Figure 4). The eight barrier island groups that skirt the Georgia coast are made up of two sets of islands formed during distinctly different geologic time periods (see Figure 7). The extremely gradual slope of the coastal plain, coupled with the high tidal range, creates the rare condition of having tidal water completely surround the set of older barrier islands immediately west of the islands fronting the ocean. In the majority of coasts, older sets of barrier islands become integrated into the mainland and only the islands fronting the ocean are the true barrier islands.

The older set of islands formed Georgia's beaches 35 to 40 thousand years ago, before the fourth and last great "Ice Age" during the late Pleistocene Epoch. Enough water was frozen during the last big freeze to lower the sea level 300 feet, exposing most of the continental shelf and placing the shoreline 50 to 60 miles offshore.

About 18 thousand years ago, at the beginning of the modern or Holocene time, continental ice sheets began to melt and the sea level rose. Sandy barrier islands near the shelf's edge rolled backward with the advancing sea level, migrating up the continental shelf. These rapidly migrating sea islands were narrow and were frequently overwashed by storms, depositing sand behind (west of) the islands. Advancing seas also transported sand around the ends of the islands. Both of these processes built the island from behind, while eroding from the front. In a phrase, islands migrated by "rolling over." Some of Georgia's smaller (Holocene) islands, such as Cabretta and Nannygoat Beaches, near Sapelo Island, are actively migrating today (see Figure 2).

Four to five thousand years ago, the rate of sea level rise greatly diminished allowing the establishment and growth of the new islands in their approximate positions today. With the exception of Jekyll and Cumberland Islands, the Holocene islands form most of Georgia's beaches. Most of the Holocene formations which fronted Jekyll and much of Cumberland have been lost to erosion, and the Pleistocene shorelines have again assumed those beaches (Figure 7).

The varied distances between the Holocene and Pleistocene islands often reflect the relative influences that the sedimentary outflow of Georgia's major rivers had on the inward migration of the Holocene islands. Notice the greater distances of Tybee, Wassaw, Little St. Simons, and Sea Islands from their Pleistocene counterparts in Figure 7. As you can see from the figure, these two groups of islands are immediately south of the largest rivers in Georgia, the Savannah and Altamaha. The copious outflow of sediments from these large rivers over the years slowed down the inward migration of these Holocene islands. Most of the other Holocene islands migrated closer to their Pleistocene counterparts because there was less sedimentary outflow to overcome from the smaller rivers.

A closer look at the islands grouping around St. Simons Island (Figure 1) reveals that the southern parts of Sea Island came closer to St. Simons, the farther it was away from the sedimentary influence of the Altamaha River. Still farther

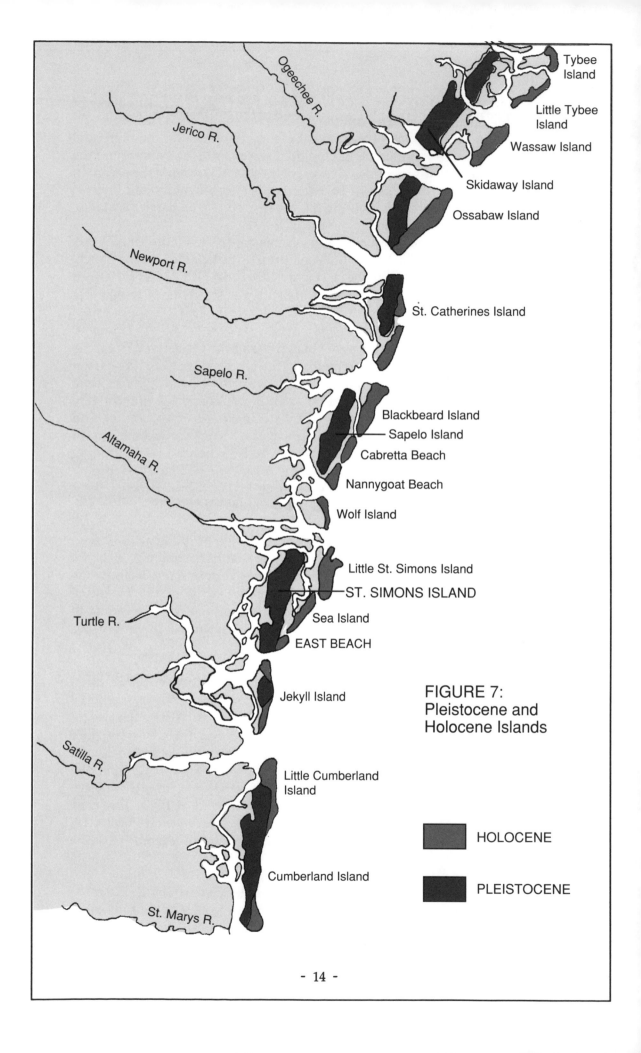

FIGURE 7:
Pleistocene and
Holocene Islands

south, two small Holocene islands, which today make up East Beach and East End, migrated even farther west. The lower end of the southern-most island, the East End fragment, joined onto the southern end of St. Simons Island. The East Beach fragment remained an island separated from the East End by an inlet, where Postell Creek (at that time called Beach Creek) flowed into the ocean. (Figure 20 shows the approximate location of the inlet.) Until the late 1920s East Beach was an island, accessible only by a bridge that spanned Postell Creek from East End. Site 5 describes the rerouting of Postell Creek and the filling in of the inlet which joined East Beach and East End as they are today.

The above described alignment of Sea Island and East Beach in relation to St. Simons Island is clearly seen from East Beach Causeway, Site 5. Figure 7 shows a similar progressive decrease in the distances between Tybee Island, Wassaw Island, and the Holocene fragment of Ossabaw Island from their Pleistocene counterparts, the farther they are located south of the Savannah River.

Today the sea level is rising at a rate of 12 to 14 inches per century and its rate of rise is increasing. The Environmental Protection Agency and many other proponents believe that the increase in rate of sea level rise is due largely to increased levels of carbon dioxide and other "greenhouse gases" from the unrestrained use of fossil fuels (gasoline and other petroleum products).[4] In spite of the global sea level rise, the growth and erosion of our barrier beaches are more influenced by shifting shoals, storm episodes, and seasonal wind and tides. The descriptions in Sites 2 through 9 show how the above forces have markedly different effects on the various areas along the four miles of St. Simons' beaches.

Paradoxically, beaches, one of Earth's most dynamic and often-dangerous environments, have become highly esteemed by people as places to live. Our insistence on erecting houses and hotels on or near ever-changing beaches has caused untold hardships and losses to us and to the beaches. The many attempts to save developed frontage and restore retreating beaches through the construction of seawalls and jetties have more often than not accelerated loss of beaches. (The destructive effects of seawalls and jetties are described in the section on Ocean Beaches and in Site 4, respectively.) More than a century of armoring and developing shorelines is seriously threatening the existence of natural, self-sustaining beaches in America.[5]

Brown Pelican
Diving

FORCES SHAPING BARRIER ISLANDS

The shapes and sizes of sandy barrier islands change constantly under the influence of winds, waves, and tidal currents. The ends of the islands are especially dynamic because of their close proximity to the inlets between the islands. Generally, the southern ends of the islands tend to accrete (build up by deposition), while the northern ends exhibit irregular growth interspersed with erosion.

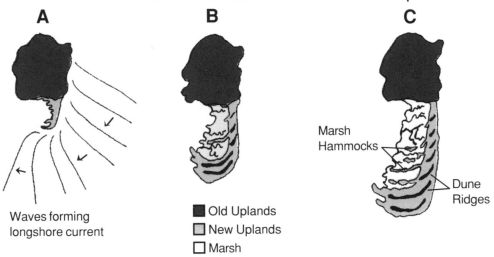

FIGURE 8: Formation and Growth of a Recurved Spit

A **B** **C**

Waves forming
longshore current

Marsh
Hammocks

Dune
Ridges

■ Old Uplands
▨ New Uplands
□ Marsh

Figure 8 diagrams the process by which the southern ends of barrier islands grow. Water currents carry sand, which is deposited in shallow areas near barrier islands as shoals and spits. Shoals are underwater bodies of sand which become exposed during low tide, and spits are shoals which attach to island or mainland shores. The diagram shows that spits continue to grow, dune ridge by dune ridge, toward the south, as longshore currents continue to deposit sand. The free ends of the spits tend to curve inward, toward the backs of the islands, because of the influence of inward-directed wave refraction. This wave refraction occurs as waves approach a beach at an angle. The part of the wave reaching the shallows first has its movement retarded because of friction with the bottom. This causes the rest of the wave, in the deeper water, to refract or swing toward the shallow area. As Figure 8 shows, waves approaching the shore at an angle tend to turn toward the beach, and when they reach the end of the island, they curl around the spit; hence, the term recurved. The water behind the newly accreted land now becomes shielded from waves. In these quieter waters, suspended sediments settle out, often forming marshes behind the newly accreted land. Good examples of land forming from recurved spits can be seen on the south ends of Jekyll and Sea Islands.[6,7] Notice in the diagram, Figure 8, that the older dune ridges eventually become broken up into marsh islands, known as hammocks. The Salt Marsh section, page 30, explains how meandering tidal creeks erode the old dune ridges over the years.

From the map in Figure 4, you see that the barrier islands of North Carolina (the Outer Bank Islands) are located close to the continental slope. Here, the nearshore waters are deep, so that waves and tides reach these islands relatively unchanged from the open ocean. Henceforth, with high wave energy and comparatively weak tidal currents, rapidly developing recurved spits often close off inlets between major islands during storms (see Figure 9). The tendency for inlet closure is an underlying cause for the Outer Bank Islands being long, with few and narrow inlets. While old inlets close, new inlets open by storm-driven waves breaking through weak areas along these long, attenuated islands. The narrowness of the Outer Bank Islands is due to erosion and overwash created by the massive waves that attack their shores.

FIGURE 9: Inlet Closure Through Recurved Spit Growth

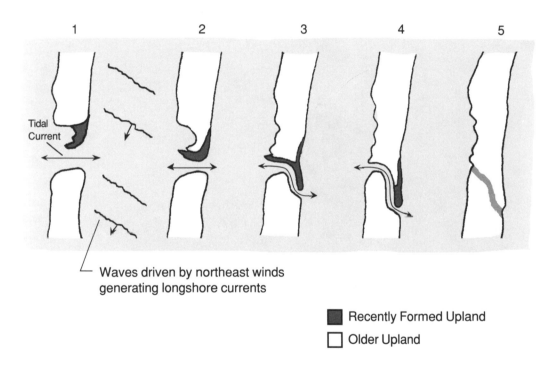

Waves driven by northeast winds generating longshore currents

■ Recently Formed Upland
☐ Older Upland

In contrast, the Georgia barrier islands, which are farther from the edge of the continental shelf, have strong tidal currents and low wave energy (see the Physical Setting section). These physical forces cause these barrier islands to be comparatively short and thick, and the inlets between them to be wide and stable (see Figure 2).

As we have seen, the extreme difference in the distances of Georgia and North Carolina from the edge of the continental shelf have created diametric wave and tide conditions, which have caused the sizes of the coastal islands and inlets to become opposite extremes. Other South Atlantic barriers with more moderate wave and tide conditions show characteristics which range between extremes of those of Georgia and North Carolina.

The northern ends of barrier islands show complex patterns of growth and erosion which vary from island to island. Tidal currents moving in and out of inlets and longshore currents moving along the face of the islands often impede one another's flow, causing suspended sand to fall out. This sedimentary sand forms shoals around the mouth of the inlets. Through southerly-directed longshore currents and wave refraction, the shoals tend to drift downward and inward toward the islands south of the inlets (see Figure 10). Waves refracting around the north-end shoals create clockwise eddies (circular currents) which tend to hold up sand, in the form of massive shoals, close to the north-end beaches. The shoals at the north end of Sea Island are a prime example of this phenomenon (see Figure 1).

FIGURE 10: Inlet Shoal System

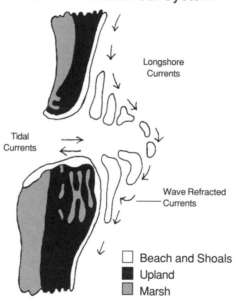

Occasionally a nearby shoal attaches itself to the northern shore of a barrier island and establishes a new beachhead which shelters the old beach from wave action. Suspended sediments fall out of the quiet waters behind the adjoining shoal, which eventually form a marsh. Any number of shoals may likewise become attached to an island, creating the often-seen corduroy pattern of ridges of upland (old beachheads) interspersed with marshes and lowlands, as shown in figure 10.

The frequent incorporation of inlet shoals onto northern beaches gives the Holocene islands of Georgia their characteristic drumstick shape. The north end of Sea Island shows this pattern of growth. Neither the accreted land on the northern ends of islands nor their associated shoals are very stable. During storms large areas of accreted land and shoals often become dislodged and are transported down along the face of the island, nourishing the beaches as they go. Site 2 describes how periodic shifting of the tidal channel of Goulds Inlet frees up shoal sand, which then migrates south, nourishing the beaches of St. Simons Island.

ECOLOGY

This section covers the four major barrier island ecosystems: ocean beach, salt marsh, maritime forest, and freshwater slough. Besides presenting a background on barrier island ecology, the descriptions in this section act as models for the comparison of similar environments on St. Simons Island and East Beach.

OCEAN BEACH

SAND MOVEMENT BETWEEN BEACH AND OFFSHORE SHOALS

Figure 11 is a profile of an accreting ocean beach in Georgia, which extends from the offshore sand bars to the edge of the maritime forest. Sand bars are elongated shoals, which parallel the beach and are formed by breaking waves . Because of the low wave energy, sand bars on Georgia beaches are not as clearly defined as those on higher-energy beaches like those in New Jersey and North Carolina. The sand on the beach dynamically interchanges with the sand from the offshore sand bars, submerged beach and inlet shoals. This dynamic interchange is often referred to as the "sand-sharing system" and is detailed in the next paragraph and diagrammed in Figure 12.

Strong onshore winds create high-energy waves which, when breaking on the beach, scour sand from the beach and dunes and deposit it on offshore bars and shoals. When surf energy is not as high, the waves gradually work sand back to the beach. Runnels, gullies parallel to the surf line, often form where the shoreward-migrating sand moves up the wet, intertidal beach. Sea breezes blow intertidal sand, which has become sufficiently dry during the lower tides, to the back beach areas where it rebuilds the upper beach and dune systems.

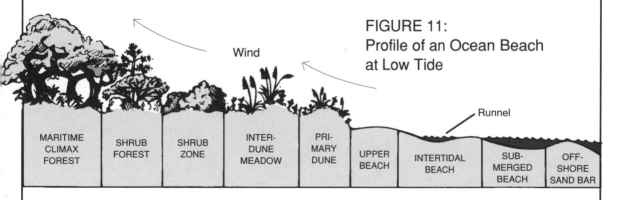

Wind

FIGURE 11:
Profile of an Ocean Beach
at Low Tide

Runnel

| MARITIME CLIMAX FOREST | SHRUB FOREST | SHRUB ZONE | INTER-DUNE MEADOW | PRI-MARY DUNE | UPPER BEACH | INTERTIDAL BEACH | SUB-MERGED BEACH | OFF-SHORE SAND BAR |

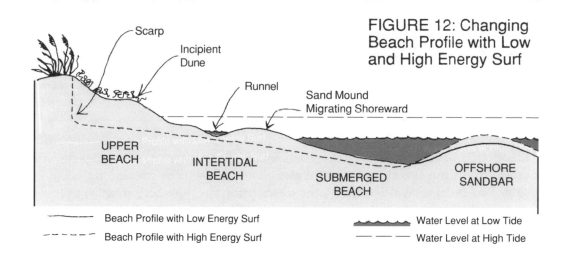

FIGURE 12: Changing Beach Profile with Low and High Energy Surf

Scarp
Incipient Dune
Runnel
Sand Mound Migrating Shoreward

UPPER BEACH
INTERTIDAL BEACH
SUBMERGED BEACH
OFFSHORE SANDBAR

———————— Beach Profile with Low Energy Surf
– – – – – – Beach Profile with High Energy Surf

Water Level at Low Tide
– – – Water Level at High Tide

Eventually, the net movement of sand between the beach and offshore-area reaches a dynamic equilibrium, only to be temporarily offset by another passing storm or an unusually high tide. Large continental storms, with their northeast winds, tend to erode the beaches in winter. Mild southerly winds and short-lived thundershowers allow beaches to build during the summer. The summer beaches are often characterized by low-lying incipient dunes which build up on the upper beach in front of a primary dune. If the beach is accreting, the incipient dunes may become a new line of primary dunes; or, as is often the case, they are swept away by one of winter's many storms (hence, the name incipient).

SEAWALLS

People often build seawalls to protect beachfront property, but such structures disrupt the sand-sharing system, often causing the beaches to disappear. When the water level is up to the seawall, the energy of the breaking waves is concentrated onto the beach in front of the wall. Since beach retreat is impossible because of the wall, erosion in that area of the beach is greatly increased.

Meanwhile, the sand reservoir in back of the wall is blocked from taking part in the sand-sharing system to mitigate the erosion. Eventually more of the intertidal beach erodes, because of the loss of sand farther up the beach and the displaced wave energy bouncing off the wall. The water covering the beach deepens, allowing larger waves to go farther up the beach before breaking. The larger waves impart more energy as they break onto the wall, scouring away more sand and exacer-

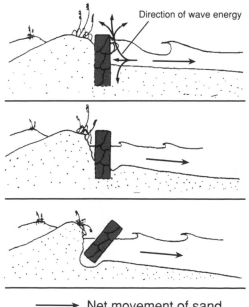

FIGURE 13:
Effect of Seawalls on Beaches

Direction of wave energy

——→ Net movement of sand

bating erosion. In most cases, this degrading cycle continues until the beach washes away. The scouring action of the waves at the base of the wall and the back erosion created by waves coming over the wall can eventually loosen the sand at the wall's underpinnings, causing the seawall to eventually sink or fall apart. The above process is depicted by Figure 13.

Seawalls are expensive to build and need constant maintenance. Hundreds of miles of America's beaches are lost due to seawalls.[5] The beaches of St. Simons Island have an extraordinary supply of sand coming from shoals surrounding Goulds Inlet. Such large supplies of sand carried in longshore currents often override the damaging effects of seawalls and, as we shall see, substantial accretion occurs on many of St. Simons' seawalled beaches.

ZONES OF THE OCEAN BEACH

The intertidal beach is the area of beach covered during high tide and exposed during the low (see Figure 11). This area of beach usually has wet, hard-packed sand. Its width is regulated by the tidal cycle and varies with the slope of the beach. Because of the gradual slope and extreme tidal range, the intertidal beaches of Georgia can extend as much as a quarter of a mile out to sea. Intertidal beaches on the north ends of islands may extend several miles offshore during low tide, due to inlet shoaling conditions mentioned on page 18 of the Geology section. Few organisms can inhabit the intertidal zone because of the intermittent exposure to air and water and because of shifting sand. The majority of intertidal

Mole Crab

residents are found either in burrows or interspersed among the wet sand grains.

The burrows of ghost shrimp and several kinds of polychaete worms can be found at the lower intertidal beach during a lower tide (see Appendix B). With certain seasons and weather conditions, algae and diatoms living in the sand often produce green and mustard hues on patches of wet beach. Coquina clams and mole crabs, moving just beneath the surface of the sand, filter out tiny planktonic organisms suspended in water thrown up onto the beach by breaking waves. Their presence is often given away by the little "V" patterns created by their tiny antennae or syphons penetrating the surface of the sand, seen below the backwash.

Moon Snail

Impressions and trails of sand dollars, moon-snails, lettered olive shells, baby's ears and other shallow-water marine organisms can be seen in the lowest intertidal areas or shallow, water-filled depressions (tide pools). Upon seeing a circular depression with the five radial indentations, slip your hand under the pattern and you will bring up a living sand dollar.

Sand Dollars

The larger of the myriad tiny creatures living among the wet sand grains can be seen by flushing the wet sand through a window screen or a household sieve. As the sand washes through with the seawater, these tiny animals, mostly amphipods, and small polychaete worms, are left wriggling on the screen. These tiny creatures living among sand grains are collectively referred to as psammon. Psammon provide food for sandpipers that busily probe the sand with their beaks at the edge of the surf.

The intertidal beach is a visiting place for many aquatic and terrestrial animals. Aquatic animals come in with the tide to feed and to escape from predators. Those that die or are left stranded by the retreating tide provide food for the many shorebirds, ghost crabs, raccoons, rats, and insects coming from the land.

The presence of many small dead fish on the beach may be from shrimp boats working offshore. They take only the shrimp and sometimes a few fish and crabs which amounts to about 10% of their catch and discard the rest. A trail of dead fish and crabs are often the leavings of some sein-ers who have little reverence for life.

Psammon

Compared to the higher-energy beaches of the Carolinas and Florida, Georgia beaches have fewer shells. Our waves often lack the energy to carry the larger shells to beaches and therefore, the shells are often deposited on the offshore shoals. Only during storms are many of the larger shells tossed onto our beaches.

The upper beach is the dry sand area between the intertidal beach and the primary dunes (see Figure 11). The upper beach is often eroded by storms or flooded during our greatest tides (spring tides) and it reappears during milder weather and lower tides (neap tides). Spring tides occur twice a month when the moon and sun are in alignment during the new or full moon. As Figure 14 shows, the waters pulled up by gravity of the sun and moon summate or add to each other, increasing the difference between the high and low tides. Neap tides occur between spring tides when the sun and moon are closer to 90-degree angles with each other during the quarter moons. The tide diagram shows that the water attracted by the sun and moon occur at different quarters of the globe, so that the differences between the high and low tides are diminished, causing the neap tide.

With such dynamics, plant growth on the upper beach is not always permanent. Plants on the upper beach during a neap tide are often inundated during the spring tide. Because of the extreme tidal range and gentle slope of the continental shelf, Georgia beaches are characterized by wide intertidal zones (wet beaches) and narrow or nonexistent upper beaches (dry beaches). Beaches with greater wave energy and smaller tides, like New Jersey, have narrower wet beaches and wider dry beaches.

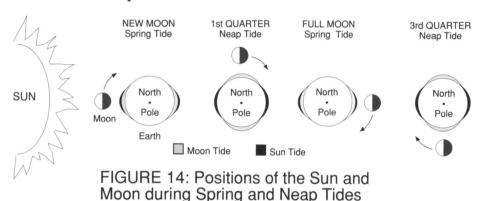

FIGURE 14: Positions of the Sun and Moon during Spring and Neap Tides

Windrows of marsh wrack (dead cordgrass stalks carried by tidal currents from the marsh) are often left along the high-tide line of the beach by the retreating wave wash. Marsh wrack provides a moist environment for beach hoppers (amphipods), insects and microorganisms. The 0.5- to 2-inch diameter holes seen near the wrack and in the dry sand of the upper beach are ghost crab burrows. Occasionally, ghost crabs can be seen out of their burrows during the day, but at night, hundreds can be seen foraging in the marsh wrack.

The marsh wrack also provides a mesh in which wind-blown sand and seeds are trapped, beginning the building process of a burgeoning new dune (incipient dune). Pioneer plants like Russian thistle, sea rocket, orach, sea-purslane, and beach croton quickly occupy the incipient dunes and dry beach behind. As was stated earlier, if the beach is accreting, these new dunes grow and develop into primary dunes. Prior to understanding the important role of marsh wrack in building dunes, some of the hotels on St. Simons used to rake up the wrack because of its "unsightliness" and found that new dunes did not appear and beach growth diminished.

Like the upper beach, primary dunes present harsh living conditions because of the salt spray, quick water drainage, shifting sand and solar radiation. These areas are often considered the "deserts" of the beach. Many resident plants of the beach have developed adaptations similar to desert plants, by having thick succulent leaves which store water and reduce surface evaporation. Some desert plants like the yucca have deep taproots which penetrate to the ground water. Most of the other beach plants, like the grasses, weeds, and shrubs, have extensive fibrous root systems which spread throughout the sand, catching water as it quickly percolates through the sand. Root competition is stringent in these shifting, nutrient-poor beach soils. A supplementary supply of plant nutrients, nitrates, phosphates, etc., come from salts left on the ground surface by the seawater spray. The high concentration of sodium chloride in the seawater, dangerous to most plants, is diluted by the rains as it and the other, more beneficial sea salts seep into the ground.

On top of and between the primary dunes, sea oats, salt meadow cordgrass, bitter panic grass, dropseed grass, and sandspur, and other grasses, grow among beach elder, pennywort (dollarweed), beach croton, yucca, and prickly-pear cactus. Sea oats are master dune builders. The long curly leaves and tall seed heads trap wind-blown sand, burying themselves and neighboring plants. By growing vertical runners to the surface of the dune, sea oats stay ahead of the accumulating sand, while most of the other competing plants become buried, die, and provide humus (decaying organic fertilizer) for the sea oats. This is why the tops of many dunes often have almost pure stands of sea oats growing on them. Because of their vital role in building and stabilizing dunes, sea oats are protected by Georgia law.

Prickly-pear
Cactus

Back from the primary dunes, many of the dune and pioneer plants gradually yield to a variety of flowering weeds, grasses, and woody plants which make this area a beach meadow. Here, the beach soils have had sufficient time to accumulate humus with the passing generations of plant and animal communities. Humus increases the soil's ability to retain water and becomes a major source of plant fertilizer. These improved soil conditions have opened the way for the colonization of the highly competitive, dry-field plants. (Progressive changes in plant communities, which accompany soil development, is known as ecological succession.)

The greatest variety of plants in this area is found in the swales, or low areas between the dunes, where the soil surface is better protected from wind and is closer to the ground water. For this reason these areas are often called interdune meadows (see Figure 11). Camphor weed, wild bean, butterfly pea, pennywort, dune primrose, spurge-nettle, muhley grass, and the brightly-colored firewheels occupy much of the flowering meadows. The taller dune ridges often continue to support sea oats and sparse communities of plants more typical of the primary dunes. Because of their higher elevation, the dune-ridge communities are exposed to winds with salt-laden mist, which severely desiccate plant tissues. Topsoil development is retarded by winds blowing away most of the decaying plant materials. Poor water retention and remoteness from the ground water keep the dune soils dry. Soil development on dunes is sufficiently retarded so that it is not uncommon to have sea oat-covered dune ridges in the midst of areas supporting shrubs and trees. Good examples of beach meadows are seen on East Beach, Site 4.

As the beach soils continue to age and develop, wax myrtles appear among meadow flowers and grasses. Wax myrtles grow into tall shrubs and eventually shade out most of the sun-loving meadow plants. Areas where wax myrtles predominate are often referred to as shrub zones.

With time and further soil development, trees, such as red cedar, Hercules' club, pine, yaupon holly, groundsel-tree, red bay, and a variety of hybrid oaks join the wax myrtles, transforming the area into a shrub forest. The trees and shrubs often become entangled in woody vines, such as cat brier, pepper vine, Virginia creeper, and muscadine grape. These wild, ragged shrub forests are a sanctuary for much of the wildlife of the back beach area.

Further back, live oak become established and grow. Eventually they form a canopy which shades out many of the shrub forest species. Wax myrtles, cedars, red bays, and hollies survive to become understory plants and the pines and some of the vines become part of the canopy of the developing maritime forest. Under the best conditions, it takes up to a century for a beach to develop a soil which can support a maritime forest.

Beaches that are eroding often lack dunes and meadows and have shrubs and even trees in the wave wash. East End Beach, Site 3, often shows this condition because of its cycle of erosion and accretion. Around developed areas, many of St. Simons' beaches are seawalled, obliterating most of the beach zonation (Sites, 7, 8 and 9).

SALT MARSH

The major salt marshes of the Georgia coast occur in shallow areas between the Holocene and Pleistocene barrier islands and between the barrier islands and the mainland (see Figure 2). The marshes are flooded by tides twice daily. The large tidal range, together with the gentle slope of the continental shelf, contributes to the extensive, four- to eight-mile-wide marshes between the mainland and the barrier islands.

The coast of Georgia is only 100 miles long, yet its one-half million acres of salt marsh constitute nearly one-third of all the salt marshes of the Eastern Atlantic States. Examples of these impressive marshes are seen from the causeways connecting St. Simons Island to the mainland and to its neighboring Holocene islands of Sea Island and East Beach (Sites 1 and 5).

The marsh is a harsh environment for most resident plants and animals. Common to all intertidal areas, intermittent exposure to air and salt water poses serious problems for resident life in the salt marsh. Rapid changes of temperature and salinity (salt concentration) that accompany tidal influx further limit resident survival. The saturated muddy soils are low in oxygen and their long hours of exposure to air tend to concentrate salt through evaporation of seawater. The degrees to which these and other limiting factors exist in the different zones of the marsh are covered in the following paragraphs. Even though relatively few species actually reside in any one place in the salt marsh, abundant suspended life drifts with the tidal waters in the creeks. Many land animals, especially birds, and aquatic life from the sounds and nearshore oceans, visit the marsh to feed and to seek shelter.

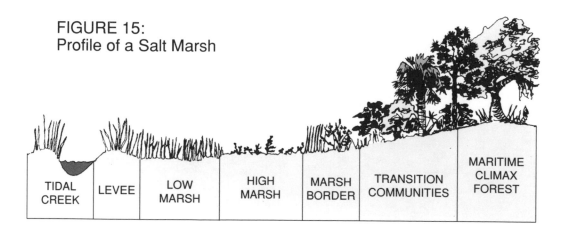

FIGURE 15:
Profile of a Salt Marsh

| TIDAL CREEK | LEVEE | LOW MARSH | HIGH MARSH | MARSH BORDER | TRANSITION COMMUNITIES | MARITIME CLIMAX FOREST |

ZONES OF THE SALT MARSH

The salt marsh can be divided into several ecological zones relative to the time and depth of tidal inundation (Figure 15). The levee marsh refers to the banks of tidal creeks. Here the soil is washed regularly with moving seawater, which minimizes changes in salinity and temperature and continually supplies nutrients to the plants along the creek banks. On the levees, smooth cordgrass usually grows to its full height of six feet.

Behind the levees is the low marsh, which composes the vast amount of the southern marshlands. The incoming tide overflows the banks of many small creeks and floods the low marsh for several hours a day. As the shallow, silt-laden water moves over the dark mud, it is heated by the sun. The increased temperature and the great quantity of detritus (suspended organic matter) in the water greatly reduce the amount of dissolved oxygen available to aquatic organisms.

Blue Crab

In the oppressive heat of the summer, fish kills occasionally occur in these poorly-circulated backwaters, and blue crabs have been observed to climb out onto mud banks to breathe, while waiting for the incoming tide. In these shallow marsh waters, the elevated temperatures contribute to the rise in salt concentration through evaporation. The above conditions, coupled with the intermittent exposure to air and water, make the low marsh at times more inhospitable than the levee marsh. Here cordgrass only grows one to three feet high.

With a slight rise in elevation, the low marsh turns into a high marsh with a sandier soil. The higher elevation allows this area to be barely covered with enough tidal water to cover its surface for an hour or less each day. The long periods of air exposure leave more time for water evaporation which further increases the salinity of the high marsh soils. The high salt concentration severely limits the growth of plants living in this area. The cordgrass is either dwarfed (three to 12 inches high) or not present. And, more salt-resistant species such as glasswort, saltwort, and salt grass populate much of the

Ribbed Mussel

high marsh. Often bare sandy areas, called "salt pans," are found where the salt concentration has become suffiniently high to inhibit all resident plant life. Concentrations of salt more than four times that of seawater commonly occur in the ground water of high marshes. It is not uncommon to see salt crystals mixed among the surface sand in a salt pan at a lower tide. Salt pans are described in Site 5.

The levee and low marshes are populated with mud fiddlers, marsh crabs (purple square-backed crabs), mud crabs, oysters, ribbed mussels, polychaete worms, periwinkle snails, and two kinds of black marsh snails. Periwinkle snails are seen moving up and down the grass stalks grazing on the algae left behind by the retreating tide. The marsh snails crawl about on the surface of the mud eating algae or anything else left behind to scavenge.

As one moves toward the higher, sandier marsh, mud fiddlers and marsh crabs give way to their counterparts, the sand fiddlers and wharf crabs (smaller, brown square-backed crabs), and the other animals mentioned above are either absent or only seen occasion- ally. The small (1/8-inch) round, sandy pellets scattered about the numerous fiddler holes (burrows) are expecto- rated from the mouths of sand fid- dlers after they have removed all of the algae and organic matter from each sand grain with their many, highly specialized mouth parts. The cleansing process usually leaves the pelleted sand whiter than the sur- rounding sand. Algae and detritus (dead organic matter) left behind by the tidal waters are the principle source of food for the fiddlers and the many other animals of the marsh food chain. The larger, darker pel- lets (1/2-inch-wide) are formed from sand excavated from the dig- ging and repairing of burrows by the fiddlers.

Sand
Fiddler

At the marsh border, where marshes meet uplands (main- land and marsh islands called ham- mocks), the ground elevation is above the high marsh and the tidal flow no longer reaches this area, except during spring and storm tides. Without the daily wash of seawater, rains and freshwater run-off from nearby uplands markedly lower salinity of the marsh border. The tall, dark needle rush and sea oxeye, whose yellow, aster flowers bloom through- out the summer, rim the marshes and hammocks, making the marsh borders visible from afar. In the fall, the light purple blossoms of the marsh lavender and marsh aster add a delicate lavender hue to the marsh border. Typical of many inter-island marshes with freshwater influence, the marshes on the east side of Sea Island Road (Site 16) are almost entirely populated by needle rush. Here a substantial amount of fresh water runs into the marsh from the surrounding uplands and many hammocks.

At a slightly higher elevation, other marginal plants such as marsh elder, groundsel-tree, and salt meadow cordgrass appear. It is interesting to note that salt meadow cordgrass or salt meadow hay (*Spartina patens*) is the predominant marsh plant of the New England and Middle Atlantic states. As the name salt meadow hay implies, it was (and to a lesser extent still is) harvested as cattle feed. The thin-blade salt meadow cordgrass gives the Northern marshes a softer textural appearance than that of the Southern marshes, which are dominated by the thicker-blade smooth cordgrass.

Purple Square-backed Crab

Among watery depressions in this less-saline area, the largest and less-frequently seen fiddler crab, the brackish-water fiddler, can be found. Brackish-water fiddlers are occasionally seen among foraging groups of sand fiddlers in the high marsh and salt pans. The only time these large fiddlers are popularly seen is when they periodically migrate in large bands across uplands. The author has received calls from surprised and somewhat intimidated Island residents inquiring about these herds of "giant" fiddlers scurrying over the roads and through their yards.

Cabbage palms are often seen fringing marshes. When present, they occupy the edge of a transition community of woody plants that precede the maritime live oak forest. Red cedar, wax myrtle, yaupon holly, red bay, and the introduced salt cedar frequent these communities. These same transition communities are seen surrounding the larger marsh hammocks. Similar to the shrub forest of the beach, marsh borders and transitional communities are favored nesting grounds for birds and feeding areas for many animals. Where an upland rises steeply above a marsh, there is little or no area for a transition community, so the maritime forest often extends to the edge of the marsh. The languid limbs of the great live oaks, laden with Spanish moss and hanging over the edge of the marsh, create a serene setting unique to Southern salt marshes.

MEANDERING TIDAL CREEKS

The water in tidal creeks is contained by mud banks (levees) which offer little resistance to erosion. Whenever there is a curve in one of these creeks, water tends to move faster on the outside of the turn and slower on the inside; much in the same way that you, walking on the outside, have to move faster around the turns of a track in order to stay up with a fellow walker on the inside. The faster-moving water tends to erode the outer part of the turn, while the slower-moving water tends to deposit sediment on the inside part of the turn. The curves in a tidal creek tend to become more exaggerated as this process continues. Experienced boaters stay close to the outer bank when going around the bend in a marsh creek where the water is the deepest, and they avoid shoals which often form off the inside bank of the turn.

Figure 16 shows that as the curve of a marsh creek erodes outward, forming a loop, the curves at the base of the loop erode inward toward each other. Eventually the curves at the base of the loop connect, breaking open a new and shorter pathway for water to flow. Seeking the path of least resistance, the shorter new pathway takes over the major flow and the longer loop is eventually bypassed. Water stranded in the loop forms temporary ponds, which eventually silt in with marsh sediments. These dormant loops, left behind by meandering

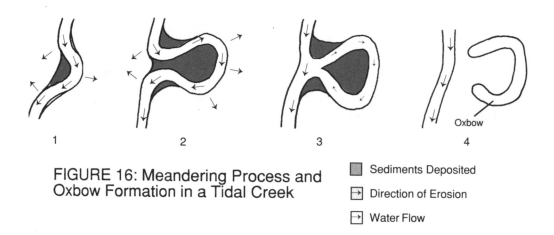

FIGURE 16: Meandering Process and Oxbow Formation in a Tidal Creek

■ Sediments Deposited

→ Direction of Erosion

→ Water Flow

creeks, are called oxbows. Old marsh creeks often leave aside many oxbows as they flow their tortuous routes, making new oxbows on the way.

Upland areas are often eroded by these migrating loops. A great part of the western side of St. Simons Island has been eroded away by the meanderings of Dunbar Creek, described in Site 16. High-bluffed uplands bordering marshes are often the tell-tale signs of erosion by a meandering creek. Much of the main garrison of Ft. Frederica, standing on a bluff on the Frederica River, has fallen into the meander it overlooks (described in Site 14).

Rows of tree-covered hammocks, seen skirting across marshes on the back-side of barrier islands, are often remains of relic dune ridges, which were cut into pieces by meandering creeks over the centuries (see Figure 17). Figure 8, which diagrams the growth of recurved spits, indicates the erosion of older dune ridges by meandering marsh creeks. An excellent example of dune ridge erosion by meandering creeks is seen in the marshes on the eastern side of St. Andrews picnic area on Jekyll Island. A description of this is seen in Area 3 of the Field Guide to Jekyll Island.[6]

Rows of little hammocks near major tidal creeks may not always be eroded dune ridges. They could be ballast islands left behind long ago by sailing ships, which unloaded ballast stones before taking on cargo. The Lumber Mill Period of the History section, page 41, describes this phenomenon and locates such ballast islands on the Frederica River, opposite the Epworth Methodist Center.

THE VITAL ROLE OF SALT MARSHES AND SHALLOW SEAS TO OCEAN LIFE

Algae and smooth cordgrass are the main food producers of the Southern marshes. Cordgrass only liberates its nutrients to the marsh after it dies and decomposes. Abundant sea life, both residential and that which drifts in and out

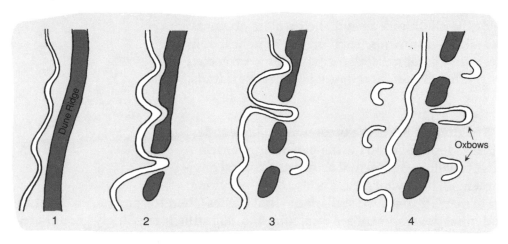

FIGURE 17: Erosion of Dune Ridges by a Meandering Tidal Creek   (sequence over centuries of time)

with the tides, feeds on these plant materials and on each other. Much of the suspended (planktonic) life is made up of fragile larval forms of many marine species, including commercial species such as shrimp, crabs, flounder, sea trout, and menhaden. The abundant suspended life and sediment load give marsh water its murky appearance which is often aptly described as "vegetable soup." Site 5 includes an excellent view of the water in a tidal creek, as seen from the East Beach Causeway bridge. A seine net pulled in a marsh creek reveals a wide variety of immature fish and invertebrates, which indicate the marsh's role as a nursery ground. After feeding and growing, many of these species mature and return off-shore to become a vital support to the food chain of the open ocean.

Larval Forms

Life in the open or pelagic ocean is spare and desert-like. Only in the top 100 to 300 feet of ocean can diatoms, one of the ocean's most abundant and important algae, grow and photosynthe-size. The pelagic oceans are on the average two miles deep. Most of the products of decay, which are the source of the algae's fertilizers, are located on the bottom. With thousands of feet of water separating the algae from most of their source of fertilizer, the pelagic algae population is kept at a stringent minimum. Since diatoms and other algae are the main producers on which animal life is dependent, sea life in the open oceans is sparse.

On the other hand, the shallower seas surrounding the continents are highly productive. In these areas the bottom is in sufficient proximity to the sun-lit waters to allow the nutrient-rich bottom sediments to reach the algae. With unleashed algal growth and photosynthesis, animal life of the shallow seas and shelf waters abounds. Coastal environments, such as salt marshes, kelp forests and coral reefs also offer shallow protected environments, which become vital nursery grounds.

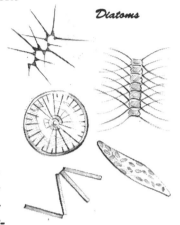

Diatoms

The diverse life in the oceans, as we have today, is totally dependent on the life-generating contributions of shallow continental oceans and coastal environments. These vital areas are also the most vulnerable to man's impact. Oil spills, industrial wastes (chemical and radioactive) and residential development are escalating and polluting increasingly greater areas of these productive ocean environments every year. New earth-centered attitudes and far-reaching management strategies need to evolve soon, if we are to preserve the present life of the oceans.

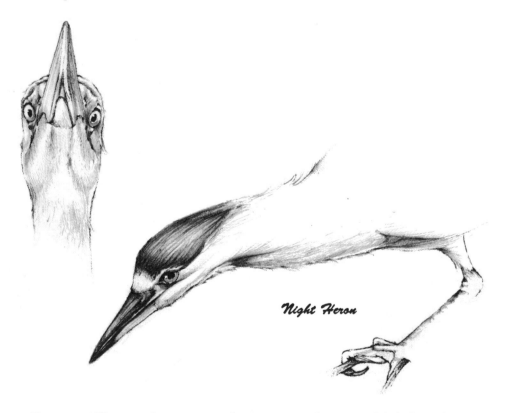

Night Heron

Herons, Egrets and Bitterns often appear to be gazing over the water while fishing; however, because of the odd placement of their eyes, they are in fact peering downward into the water.

MARITIME FOREST

The maritime live oak forest is the predominant climax community of the southeastern barrier islands. This means that, under prevailing physical and climatic conditions, the climax community propagates itself and tends to remain relatively unchanged over time. Other less-stable communities such as beaches, marshes, shrub forests, and sloughs (wet freshwater lowlands) tend to ultimately succeed to maritime forests, barring any natural or man-caused disruptions. (See Ocean Beach, page 24, for an explanation of ecological succession.) The fact that the maritime forest is the major climax community explains why these forests often occupy the oldest areas of barrier islands.

These low, dense, gray-green forests cover most of the uplands of the barrier islands. The larger trees, such as live oaks, Southern magnolias, pines, and cabbage palms, intertwined by numerous woody vines, form the canopy. The canopy shades and shelters forest life and retains moisture in the forest soils and air. Shrubs and smaller trees, such as red bay, yaupon holly, American holly, sparkleberry, laurel cherry and wax myrtle form the understory beneath the canopy. The canopy and understory provide abundant nesting sites and runways for birds, squirrels and other arboreal creatures. Saw palmettos, woods flowers, ferns, and younger generations of shrubs and trees form the ground cover. The never-ending shower of nuts, fruits, leaves, rotting bark and branches feed the wild animals of the forest and contribute to the accumulating litter on the forest floor.

Wild Cucumber

It is surprising that the maritime forest, especially on the younger barrier islands, is supported by such nutrient-poor, sandy soils. The high humidity, coupled with the long summers of 90-plus-degree temperatures, facilitates rapid decay of the dead materials on the forest floor. In this way plant nutrients are continually replenished. Most of the trees of the forest have shallow, wide-spreading root systems which quickly glean nutrients from the rain water as it percolates through the decaying leaf litter. (Site 13 further discusses root adaptations of live oaks.) The poor island soils, then, are compensated by the rapid turnover of nutrients throughout the maritime forest community.

If a maritime forest is totally destroyed, it requires centuries for the soil to again be able to support a climax forest. Without the network of roots and the shelter of the trees, the thin layer of topsoil is easily carried off by winds and water. Without the trees and arboreal life to supply the soil with dead leaves, feces, and other organic fallout, the raw materials for the building of a topsoil are lost. Only the hardiest of plants, similar to those found in beach meadows, can grow on the remaining sand; and from there begins the slow, tortuous process of plant succession leading to the eventual development of a maritime forest.

When fires burn live oak forests, loblolly and slash pines often take over, due to their rapid growth rate and ability to grow in poor, fire-cooked soils. Unlike oaks and other hardwoods, pine forests are unable to succeed themselves without frequent occurrence of natural fires or clear cutting and replanting of pines by man. The young, sun-dependent pines cannot grow in the shade of the parent trees. Shade-tolerant hardwoods, however, do grow among the large pines and quietly wait for the great pines to fall over from old age or disease, before they take over.

On the other hand, hardwoods are easily destroyed by fire, while pines have evolved extraordinary fire-resistant adaptations. Pines are insulated from the fire's heat by air trapped in their thick, loosely layered bark. When the outer layers of the bark are burning, they curl up and fall to the ground, carrying the hot embers away from the tree. When mature, the pine's 90- to 120-foot-high crowns are well out of reach of the flames of most forest fires in the Southeast. In areas where fires are frequent, pine forests predominate and are sometimes referred to as "fire climaxes." Man often simulates the fire climax condition by setting controlled fires to his cultivated pine forests to keep down the hardwood undergrowth.

Maritime forests on older barrier islands and on the coastal mainland have richer soils and a greater diversity of species. Water oak, laurel oak, pignut hickory, red maple, tulip and sweetgum are added to the list of maritime forest species. Examples of these older-island forests are found along Frederica Road, Site 11.

FRESHWATER SLOUGH

Freshwater sloughs come in many forms, from temporary ponds to large permanent ponds and swamps. Sloughs occur where the surface of the ground reaches down to the water table. Many sloughs on Holocene barrier islands originate in the swales, or the low areas between the dunes, where there are sufficient clay sediments to hold water. If the beach has been accreting over the years, the same slough may be surrounded by a changing succession of beach-plants and eventually end up in a maritime forest. Sloughs undergo their own successions, dependent on their age, permanency during drought, exposure to sun and the kinds of environments in which they are located. Two sloughs in different zones of East Beach, supporting entirely different plant communities, are described in Site 4.

Sloughs may originate from segments of marsh creeks that have lost their tidal flow. (The meandering section of the Salt Marsh, page 30, describes this type of slough formation in connection with oxbows.) As upland succession takes place in these stranded marsh areas, the old creek beds often develop into freshwater sloughs. With time the larger sloughs may succeed into swamps, large ponds supporting lowland forests. These lowland forests, with their dense stands of bay, red maple, tupelo, and water oak, contrast markedly with the upland maritime forest in the midst of which they are often found. The system of ponds seen from Frederica Road near Christ Church appears to have been formed from stranded areas of the Dunbar Creek marsh. A good example of a lowland swamp forest is found in the Woodland Walk section of Site 13.

Whitetop Sedge

Sloughs are an important source of fresh water for the wildlife of a barrier island, especially during periods of drought. The deeper, shaded, maritime forest sloughs often have water long after other island sloughs have dried up, making them crucial freshwater reserves. In the past decade, the greater incidences of drought have caused even these sloughs to become dry, creating hardship for all of the island's wildlife. Seasonal fluctuation of water level in sloughs causes the death of many water-dependent plants and animals. The accumulating dead organisms and leaf litter, moldering in the sloughs, are a major contributor of nutrients in the surrounding soils.

Sloughs add greatly to the diversity of island wildlife by providing a habitat for many forms of freshwater-dependent species, such as freshwater fish, amphibians, water snakes, the many insects whose life cycles require fresh water, and a variety of aquatic plants. Sloughs are critical environments for

Georgia's heron, egret, ibis and wood stork rookeries. They provide nesting and feeding grounds for waterfowl, many songbirds and a variety of other animals. Because of the abundance of life surrounding sloughs, many larger predators such as alligators, cottonmouth moccasins, rattlesnakes, raccoons, opossums and bobcats are also attracted. Alligators that have taken up residence in a slough often become "keepers of the hole" by digging out sloughs whose water level has dropped below the ground during droughts. As a result, ground water is again exposed and, gratefully, made available to the other animals.

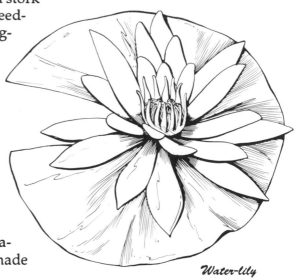

Water-lily

In contrast to the quiet stillness of the salt marsh on a summer evening, the presence of a freshwater slough is broadcast by the cacophony of innumerable frogs, toads, and peepers.

HISTORY

St. Simons Island has a rich history. This section presents a brief outline of St. Simons' history, mainly to account for the human influence on the island's natural environments. The history books listed in Appendix C present a more complete coverage.

THE INDIANS OF COASTAL GEORGIA

The oldest remnant of Indian activity on the Georgia coast is the Sapelo Island shell ring, which is dated back to 5,800 years ago. The ring of oyster shells is ten to twelve feet tall and about one half the area of a football field. It is believed to be a kitchen midden (refuse pile). At the time of the Spanish discovery of the Georgia coast in 1540, the Creek Indians occupied the barrier islands and much of the coastal mainland. According to Edwin Green, the Creeks were tall, well shaped and had a peaceful countenance.[8] They hunted, fished and cultivated corn, melons, squash, beans, tobacco and fruit. The large piles of oyster shells, such as the Sapelo shell ring and others encountered on the barrier islands, testify to the Indians' appetite for oysters.

SPANISH MISSION PERIOD (1560 to 1680)

While the Spanish occupied this part of the new world, great efforts were made to convert the Indians to Christianity and to take control of their lands and villages. Incompatible lifestyles and beliefs between the Europeans and Indians led to much misunderstanding, strife and martyrdom. Through the perseverance of the Spanish missionaries, the missions grew for 70 to 80 years.

In the late 1590s, three missions were established on St. Simons Island: Asao, near Ft. Frederica; Ocotonico, between the lighthouse and Frederica River; and Santo Domingo de Talaxe, near Butler Point. Toward the end of the 1600s, Indian

The Georgia Martyrs

In 1597 five Franciscan missionaries were martyred.

uprisings, pirate raids and disease led to the decline and eventual disappearance of the Indians and Spanish missions in Georgia. Some of the unrest was spurred on by the British, who infiltrated into Georgia from their colony in Charleston, South Carolina. For a period of about 50 years, after the Spanish withdrew to Florida, a remnant population of Indians was all that remained on St. Simons, Jekyll and Sea Islands, until the arrival of the English colonists.

THE BRITISH COLONIAL PERIOD (1730 to 1780)

At the beginning of this period, the Spanish had a stronghold in Florida and the British had colonies as far south as the Charleston area. The land between, which included the Georgia coast, was an area of ambiguous title and became the site of territorial conflict between the Spanish and British for more than a decade. In 1733 a British colony was established in Savannah and, three years later, Ft. Frederica and Ft. St. Simons were settled on St. Simons Island, under the leadership of James Oglethorpe. Ft. Frederica is described in Site 14 and Ft. St. Simons is marked by a small monument located on Ocean Boulevard between Seventh and Ninth Streets.

Three years after the British declared war on Spain in 1739, the Spanish arrived on St. Simons' shores with 52 ships and more than 3,000 men. Edwin Green tells the most extraordinary account of how Oglethorpe, with 630 men, defeated and drove off the entire Spanish army and armada through cunning, bravery and discipline.[8]

The defeat of the Spanish in the Battle of Bloody Marsh (hence, the name Bloody Marsh) sealed the fate that Georgia and the territories to the north would be of British heritage and English language instead of Spanish. Site 10 locates Bloody Marsh Monument, where the Battle of Bloody Marsh was believed to have been fought. Site 14 points out Ft. Frederica National Monument where there are the ruins of the fort and an excellent display of the history of these times.

Shortly after the disbandment of the British troops, the town of Ft. Frederica had outlived its purpose and so was abandoned shortly after the fire of 1758. Various estates on St. Simons Island were awarded to British soldiers for their service in the military. However, many of the British landowners returned to their mother country at the onset of the Revolutionary War.

PLANTATION PERIOD (1780 to 1860)

For close to a century, the Georgia coast was intensely logged and cultivated. Live oak was in great demand for shipbuilding from the middle 1700s to early 1800s. The "Of Men and Live Oaks" section of Site 13 describes the fashioning of live oaks into ship timbers and the decimation of the live oak forests on the barrier islands of the Southeast.

Cotton

The invention of the cotton gin, which eliminated the slow and laborious task of hand-picking the seeds from the cotton, greatly increased cotton production. At this time the Industrial Revolution in England came into full swing, allowing mass production of textiles by steam-powered mills. The increase of both supply and demand made cotton the major crop of the South.

The barrier islands of Georgia were of special interest to cotton growers because the island soils and sea breezes provided the necessary conditions for the successful cultivation of the highly prized Sea Island cotton, an especially long-fibered cotton which was imported from the Caribbean island of Anguilla in 1786.

St. Simons Island had 14 plantations. The approximate locations of some of these plantations are shown in Figure 18. The six greatest plantations were: Hamilton, Retreat, Hampton, Cannon's Point, Kelvin Grove and Black Banks. Notice that several locations on St. Simons Island still retain their plantation names.

Cotton was the staple crop of most of the plantations and other crops were grown to support the plantations. The grand lifestyle of these plantations is legendary and is described in the history books listed in Appendix C. Between logging for ship timbers and clearing for cotton fields, most of St. Simons' trees were cut down. Today most of the island's forests are made up of moderate-sized trees that grew after cotton farming was discontinued, following the Civil War. Site 11 points out a large forested area where cotton fields once were.

Day Flower

Edwin Green mentions that the era of the plantations started to decline sometime between 1825 to 1835.[8] Below are some of the major factors that contributed to the decline. The heirs that took over these beloved plantations lacked the fervor of the original owners. At a time when cotton production was peaking, the demand and price of cotton declined. England was having a recession and the docks were backed up with cotton bales. The plantation soils were becoming exhausted. Cotton quickly drained the soil of its nutrients and cotton growers did not practice soil conservation. The destruction of cotton crops by the boll weevil was rampant. National controversy about slave labor and new laws prohibiting importation of more slaves from Africa escalated the

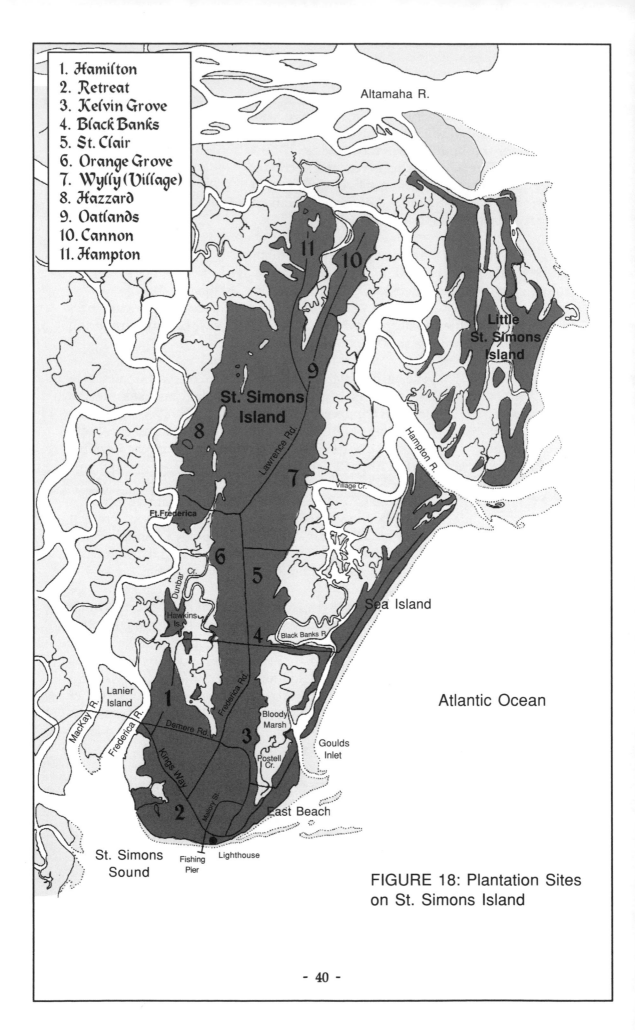

1. Hamilton
2. Retreat
3. Kelvin Grove
4. Black Banks
5. St. Clair
6. Orange Grove
7. Wylly (Village)
8. Hazzard
9. Oatlands
10. Cannon
11. Hampton

FIGURE 18: Plantation Sites on St. Simons Island

prices for slaves and unrest on the plantations. The plantations could not operate without slaves. The Civil War, which destroyed many of the antebellum homes and properties and freed the slaves, brought the final blow to the already deteriorating plantations.

THE LUMBER MILL PERIOD (1870 to 1900)

This period had its start with the growing demand for Southern lumber. Having the Altamaha River to the north and the Satilla River to the south, St. Simons Island became the ideal site for lumber mills. Four lumber mills and massive docking facilities were erected along Gascoigne Bluff on the Frederica River (the present location of the Epworth Methodist Center and the Gisco shrimp docks (see Figure 19). Cypress, pine and oak were cut mainly from the flourishing mainland forests and the logs were floated down the Altamaha and Satilla Rivers to these mills, where they were sawed into lumber for export.

Great schooners came to Gascoigne to purchase and carry the lumber to all parts of the world. Before loading up with lumber, the schooners had to dump their ballast stones. Ballast stones were carried in the holds of the empty schooners so they would ride lower and more stably on the open seas. The piles of ballast stones formed the three marsh islands (ballast islands) across the river from the Epworth Center. (Site 1 points out the ballast islands as seen from the F.J. Torras Causeway.) Margaret Davis Cate described *Saltcedar* saltcedar and the other non-native plants that grew on the piles of ballast rock, which came from seeds picked up with the stones from foreign soils. For this reason she called the ballast islands "Little Europe."[9]

On a trip across the causeway, or while visiting the Epworth Center, you might have noticed that the ballast islands are located more than a hundred feet back from the river bank, which might shed doubt on their origin, being ballast rocks heaved off the decks of the large schooners. Since the hammocks are located near the bank of the inside bend of the Frederica River, we would expect, from our understanding of the meandering process of tidal creeks, that sediments would build up in front of these islands over time. (See Salt Marsh section, page 29, for an explanation of meandering.)

Conversely, by the same process, we may understand why Epworth's banks on the outside of the bend are eroding, creating the scarped appearance from whence comes the name Gascoigne Bluff. Some of the rocks used in erosion control on Epworth's banks are ballast stones.

Today tamarisk or saltcedar, one of the plants Margaret Davis Cate described growing on the ballast islands, has naturalized and spread throughout many of the marsh hammocks in Glynn County. Saltcedars derive their name from their affinity for water, which they greedily take up at the expense of the other native plants and thus, tend to take over the hammocks they occupy.

Homes, churches, stores and a school sprang up to serve the more than 300 people associated with the mills at Gascoigne. Jewtown, the settlement on Demere Road between Frederica and Sea Island Roads (see Figure 19), was the location of a general store and residences for many of the mill workers. (Lovely Lane Chapel, the schoolhouse and some homes from the 'Mill Days' are still standing at Epworth today.) After a brief period of about 30 years, the mills closed down when the good timber was depleted. The Arthur J. Moore Museum at the Epworth Methodist Center has excellent displays depicting the Lumber Mill Period.

Over this same period, St. Simons Island, with its mild temperatures, sea breezes, beaches and beautiful live oaks, was being discovered for its vacation potential.

RESORT PERIOD (1870 to 1920)

St. Simons and other barrier islands have been vacation homes for the wealthy for many years. Unlike many of the other barrier islands which were owned by a few elite people, St. Simons offered great possibilities as a resort island because it was under the ownership of many people. With the development of a pier and ferry service from the mainland, hotels and numerous summer cottages emerged in and near the Village area, Site 9.

A trolley shuttled passengers between the pier and the St. Simons Hotel, which was in the Massengale area, Site 6. The trolley ran on Railroad Avenue, which is now Beachview Drive (see Figure 19). The activities of the islanders pulsed with the schedule of the ferries running back and forth to the mainland. In her book, *More Fun Than Heaven*, Francis Peabody McKay gives a delightful, personal account of the lives of the summer residents on St. Simons Island during this charmed period.[10]

Although the time periods of the lumber mills and the early part of the resort period overlapped, the people in the two areas had little contact. There was much wilderness and few roads between the two locations and the lifestyles and interests of the people had little in common.

With the advent of the opening of the F. J. Torras Causeway in 1924, the quiet life around the ferry dock quickly gave way to the greater independence and mobility that came with automobiles and improved roads. Shortly after the Torras Causeway opened, the Sea Island Causeway was built and the Cloister, Sea Island's resort hotel, was opened in 1928. Clusters of cottages appeared along East Beach and Butler Avenue, near the village, and other areas of the island were developed later.

RESIDENTIAL PERIOD (1930 to Present)

From the 1930s through the 1950s, many of the summer cottages became permanent homes and neighborhoods sprang up throughout the southern half of St. Simons Island. By the 1970s full-scale development began on the north end of the island. Today, residential development, property values and population on St. Simons Island are continuing to grow. St. Simons' population in the 1960s was about 6,000; in the 1970s, 7,000; in the 1980s, 9,000; and in 1992, as this book is being written, the population is about 14,000.

The island is rapidly reaching a critical level of growth and development, whereby only through careful planning involving all interest groups is St. Simons going to preserve her individualistic, natural charm.

Lady St. Simons

Lady St. Simons, she sits by the sea,
Veiled in her gray-green, live oak canopy.
A queen among beauties which close to her surround,
The sandy barrier islands of Georgia abound.

Old timers recall many the day
When nothing blocked the sunlight's way
For cotton fields spread over the ground
And timbers for ships left few trees around.

The plantation era was soon to recede
When man wore her soils and fell into need,
Ship timbering collapsed with the last great tree.
Lady St. Simons bore the wounds of man's greed.

As forest replaced the plantation fields
Covering the scars as she healed,
And people came for the sand and the sea
In the shade of her lovely, moss-covered trees.

Can we safeguard what nature has designed?
The sheer beauty that enchanted mankind,
The sublimity that surpasses all time,
Can we live with an island more naturally inclined?

Taylor Schoettle

STUDY SITES

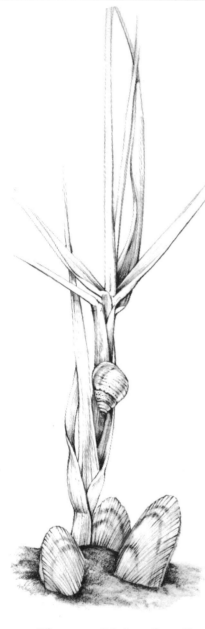

1   F. J. Torras Causeway

2. Goulds Inlet

3. Coast Guard Beach

4. East Beach

5. East Beach Causeway

6. Massengale Park

7. King & Prince

8. St. Simons Beach

9. Fishing Pier

10. Bloody Marsh Monument

11. Mid-island Forests

12. Harrington

13. Christ Church

14. Fort Frederica

15. Taylor's Fish Camp

16. Sea Island Road

There are 16 sites described in this guide to be visited. The sites were chosen for the phenomena they show and their accessibility to the public. The sites have been arranged in order to provide continuity of subject matter and to minimize travel. The sites may be visited out of sequence, but you need to be aware that some information relating to a later site may have been given in a previous one. The frequent cross-referencing of sequential information among the sites should be helpful in such circumstances. Although most people may use an automobile to visit the sites, you may find that bicycling the bike paths from site to site, where they are reasonably close together, could add to your pleasure.

Study Site Locations:

Sixteen study sites on St. Simons

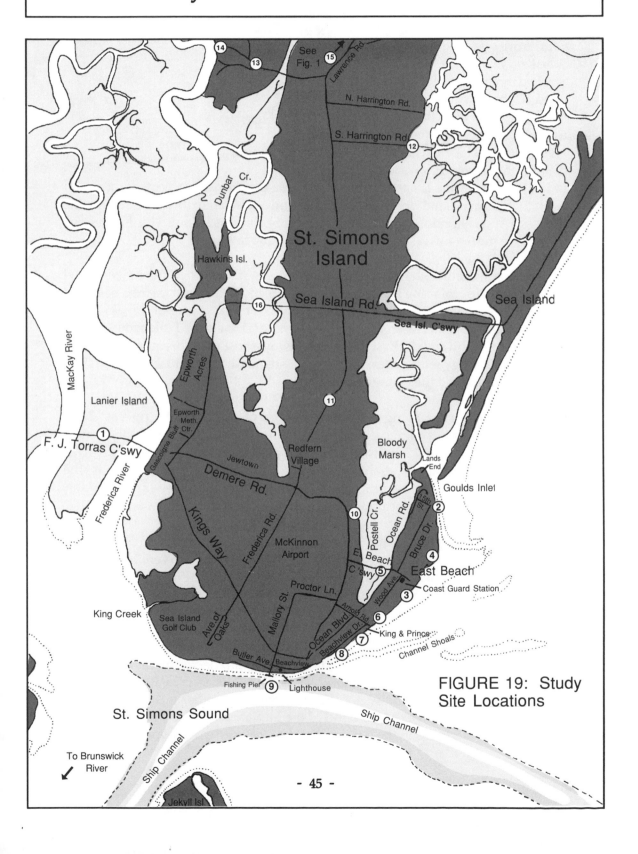

FIGURE 19: Study Site Locations

Site #1: F. J. Torras Causeway

Areas: Traversing the marshes between the mainland and St. Simons Island

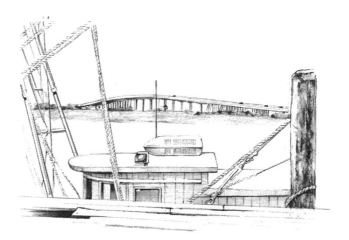

The city of Brunswick sits on one of the ancient Princess Anne barrier islands, whose shorelines were washed by the Atlantic Ocean 60 to 80 thousand years ago (see Figure 6). With the continued fluctuation of the sea level, the Pleistocene Island of St. Simons formed seaward of the Princess Anne Islands and took over the beaches. For about 40 thousand years St. Simons Island fronted the beaches and a salt marsh formed between the Princess Anne shoreline and the back side of St. Simons Island. This is the four-mile-wide marsh traversed by the F.J. Torras Causeway.

Approximately four thousand years ago, with another major sea level fluctuation, the Holocene Islands of East Beach and Sea Island formed seaward of St. Simons Island and took over the beaches. The same marsh-development process took place between St. Simons Island and the new Holocene Islands. Both the Sea Island and the East Beach Causeways cross over this marsh. The first part of the Geology section describes in more detail the barrier island formation which accompanied the changes in sea level.

Highway 17 runs along close to the edge of the ancient Princess Anne shoreline as it passes along the eastern border of the Brunswick city limits. Traveling on Highway 17, between the Sidney Lanier Bridge and the F. J. Torras Causeway, provides an excellent view of St. Simons and Jekyll Islands across the marsh. The Brunswick Visitors Center at the foot of the causeway has maps, brochures, and tourist information on Brunswick and the Golden Isles.

As you drive the F. J. Torras Causeway towards St. Simons Island, you cross over five tidal rivers. You can recognize the two navigable rivers by the high concrete bridges spanning them. The Mackay River, with the 65-foot span, is the Intercoastal Waterway and the Back River, with the 40-foot span, is the alternate route.

As you approach St. Simons Island, the Epworth Methodist Center and the St. Simons Marina are on the left and the Gisco shrimp docks are on the right of the causeway. This section of shoreline along the Frederica River is called Gascoigne Bluff. This is the site of the 19th-century lumber mills and wharfs, mentioned in the Lumber Mill Period of the St. Simons Island History section. The three marsh islands to the left, across the river from the Epworth Methodist

Center are islands produced from the great schooners offloading ballast stones before taking on lumber from the mills. It might, however, appear odd that these islands are located so far back from the river bank to be "ballast islands" (see the above-mentioned history section for an explanation).

The drive over the causeway avails an unobstructed view of a beautiful expanse of marsh, whose moods continually change with time of day, seasons and weather.

The Moods of the Marsh

The moods of the marsh constantly change
As winds and shadows move over the range
Bringing life to the grasses and rippling the bay.
The symphony of a summer's day.

As day draws to the afternoon
Mounting breezes promise a climax soon.
Slate-gray skies appear in the west
Where glorious thunderheads gather in its chest.

Like great sailing ships they glide over the plain
Spawning ripping winds and pelting rain.
Another concert ends for another day
While crossing over the causeway.

H. E. Taylor Schoettle

BEACHES OF ST. SIMONS ISLAND

FIGURE 21:
Shoreline Changes
from 1860 to 1974
(Adopted from: Griffin & Henry, 1984) [11]

■ Erosion
▨ Accretion

Approximately 4.2 miles of sandy beach skirts the southern end of St. Simons Island from Goulds Inlet to King Creek. Looking at Figure 20, one can see that the same wind, waves and tidal currents strike each area of St. Simons Island's beach from different directions and with varying intensities. The view from the St. Simons Lighthouse (Site 9) allows one to see the ever-changing directions of the beach. It should not be surprising, then, to find that different sections of St. Simons Island beach have distinctly different histories and patterns of growth and erosion. The five sections of St. Simons' beach are identified below and their positions are illustrated in Figure 20.

1. Goulds Inlet Beach - the land north of Goulds Inlet Park
2. East Beach - Goulds Inlet to the Coast Guard Station
3. East End Beach - Coast Guard Station to the King and Prince Hotel
4. St. Simons Beach - King and Prince Hotel to the Fishing Pier
5. St. Simons Sound Beach - Fishing Pier to King Creek.

Griffin and Henry reveal that similar growth and erosion patterns in these same basic areas have been occurring for over a century; albeit, they divide the beach into four sections rather than five (Figure 21).[11] The features and histories of these five sections of St. Simons Island beach are detailed in Sites 2 through 9.

FIGURE 20:
The Five Sections of St. Simons Island Beach which Show Individual Patterns of Growth and Erosion

1. Goulds Inlet Beach   4. St. Simons Beach
2. East Beach   5. St. Simons Sound Beach
3. East End Beach

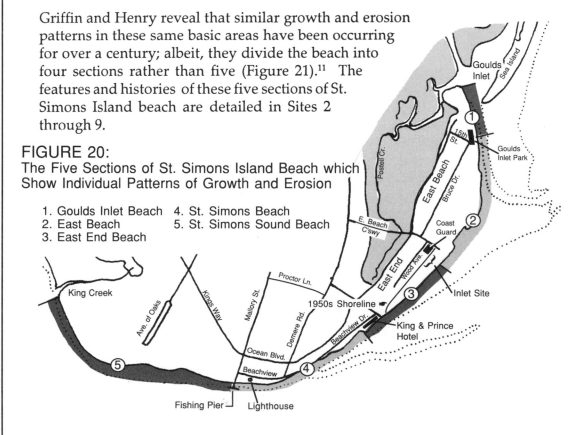

Site #2: Goulds Inlet

Areas: Goulds Inlet Park and upper East Beach

Goulds Inlet Park is located at the end of Bruce Drive where it intersects with Fifteenth Street in East Beach. Facing northeast from the parking area, you see the southern tip of the Sea Island Spit across the inlet. From this perspective, it is difficult to believe that the spit extends one-and-a-half miles down from where the Cloister (the terra-cotta roofs visible in the distance) is located.

The developed shoreline north of the park is the Land's End Subdivision (see Figure 19). The houses sit on the remaining fragment of upland that has undergone over a century of erosion. Between 1860 and 1974, 1,640 feet of land were lost along Goulds Inlet's inner shore, due to over a mile of southward growth of the Sea Island Spit (see Figure 21).[11]

The spit continued to grow, narrowing the inlet and accelerating the tidal flow through its channel. To protect the lands bordering the inlet from further loss, the rip-rap or rock seawall you see skirting the park and the Land's End beaches, was constructed in 1965. This is the northern segment of the seawall ordered by President Lyndon Johnson to be constructed along much of St. Simons Beach after Hurricane Dora in 1964. It is popularly referred to as the "Johnson Rocks." Today, the swiftly moving tidal water crowds and deeply scours the seawall, causing concern for its longevity.

As you walk south along the beach, observe the tidal wrack (mats of dead marsh grass) lying at the base of the concrete rubble wall, which fronts the houses to the right. The wrack is deposited by the high tide wash, which now regularly broaches the Johnson Rocks to the left. The small marsh area, behind the rip-rap seawall, has formed out of the mud and fine sand settling out from the seawater, forming a tide pool behind the rocks during the high tide. The rocks protect the marsh from the scouring action of the waves.

The massive shoal, drifting down from the Sea Island Spit, has been growing rapidly over the years and now extends for a half-mile from the spit beach to the middle of East Beach (see Figure 19). During high tide, most of the shoal may be under water, but its presence is revealed by the many small waves breaking on top of the shoal. Most of the tidal flow from Goulds Inlet courses between East Beach and the shoal and then flows out to sea through inlet channels, which cut across the shoal. The positions of these channels change every 10 to 30 years, affecting the erosion and accretion cycles of some of the beaches down-current of the inlet.[12]

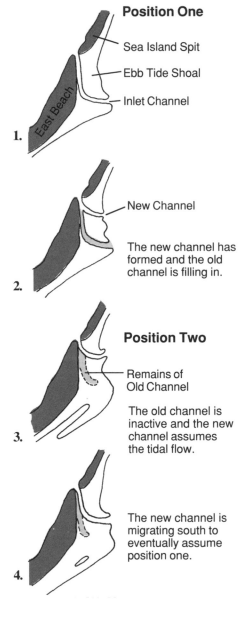

The periodic changes of the inlet channel and accompanying growth and erosion of the down-current beaches approximate the pattern described below. Position 1 in Figure 22 occurs when the main inlet channel runs for a considerable distance along the face of East Beach before turning out to sea. Under these circumstances, much of the southerly migrating sand from Sea Island is held up on the up-current or north side of the channel. And, much of the sand that is swept into the channel currents is carried sufficiently far offshore to place it outside of the longshore currents. Such conditions interrupt sand transport to the down-current beaches of St. Simons Island, contributing to their erosion. The beaches most affected are the East End and St. Simons Beaches (see Figure 20). During these times, the tidal channel is steep, wide and full of fast-moving water, making swimming along the north area of East Beach hazardous.

Periodically, other inlet channels break through the shoals closer to the tip of the Sea Island Spit (Step 2). One of these new channels with its more direct, shorter course, assumes the greater part of the tidal flow, leaving the old channel to eventually dry up (Position 2). In this configuration, the shoals to the north, formerly impounded by the old channel, are free to join the East Beach shoals below. The addition of inlet sand to the East Beach shoals allows more sand to be transported to the beaches to the south. During these times, East End and St. Simons Beaches tend to grow.

FIGURE 22: Position Changes and Migration of Goulds Inlet Channels

Over time, the new channel gradually droops southward, under the influence of the longshore currents and the meandering of the channel (Step 4). Eventually, the channel resumes a Position 1 configuration. In this position the channel again tends to block the southerly flow of sand and the down-current beaches begin to erode. Aspects of the resulting intermittent erosion and accretion of East End and St. Simons Beaches are described in Sites 4, 6, 7, and 8.

As you walk further along East Beach, notice that the beach begins to extend seaward of the Johnson Rocks and the wall appears to gradually drift up the beach, where it ends among the sand dunes between Tenth and Eleventh Streets. This indicates a southeastern shift in orientation of the shoreline, since the building of the wall in 1965.

Along with the seawall, the houses also fall back away from the beach. (See illustration below.) Most of the original houses on East Beach were built in the middle 1930s. In those days the houses were beachfront. Except for isolated episodes of erosion, most of East Beach has had a history of growth from that time to the present. East Beach has had its greatest growth toward the south as reflected by the progressively greater distance between the houses and the beach, as you walk south. The greatest extent of growth of all of St. Simons' beaches has occurred at the south-central section of East Beach.

Most of East Beach has no access by car, but can be approached on foot or by bicycle from either Goulds Inlet Park or from the Coast Guard Beach. Because the overall walking distance to the center of East Beach is shorter from the Coast Guard Beach, you may wish to return to Goulds Inlet Park and drive your vehicle to the Coast Guard Beach parking area and follow directions in Site 3. The alternative would be to continue walking south along East Beach toward the Coast Guard Beach. If you go this way, you may want to return to the Goulds Inlet park by Bruce Drive and Ocean Road. This takes you through the quaint neighborhood of East Beach and along Bloody Marsh.

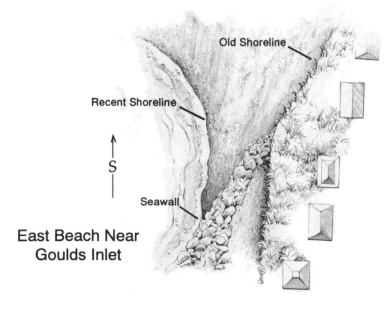

Old Shoreline

Recent Shoreline

S

Seawall

East Beach Near Goulds Inlet

Site #3: Coast Guard Beach

Areas: South end of East Beach and East End Beach

Park near the entrance of the public parking area across from the Coast Guard Station driveway. As you face toward the ocean, the houses and shrub meadow on the left side of the parking area are on the southern end of the East Beach subdivision described in Site 2.
The Coast Guard Station and the original houses on the southern end of East Beach were built in the 1930s. At that time most of them were frontage properties. Except for the extreme southern and northern ends, East Beach has had a history of growth from that time to the present.

In the early 1950s, East End Beach from the King and Prince Hotel to the Coast Guard Station and the first block or so of East Beach subdivision retreated. This left the shoreline within 50 feet of the Coast Guard Station and up to the property lines of the neighboring East Beach houses (see 1950s shoreline in Figure 20). The large shrub-covered dune in back of the older house, across the parking area from the Coast Guard Station, is a remnant of the 1950s beach. The 1950s shoreline of the East End tract to the south is approximately one block seaward of the larger trees on the other side and behind the Coast Guard Station.

Passion Flower

As you walk toward the beach, the abundance of large trees and shrubs in the shrub meadow to the left is evidence that this part of East Beach accreted quickly, to allow enough time for that extent of growth. Old aerial photographs show that in the late l950s the beach had reached the area where the first visible relic dune ridge appears, opposite the bathhouse.

The second dune ridge over which the boardwalk crosses was produced in the middle 1960s, possibly by Hurricane Dora in 1964. This placed the shoreline about 2/10 of a mile from the Coast Guard Station. Growth of this beach continued until 1986 when the shoreline grew another 1/10 of a mile beyond the crossover. Since then the beach has been slowly retreating to its present position (at the time this guide is being written) where the high tide waves again are washing the 1960s dune line.

If you are visiting the sites in sequence and have not yet explored East Beach, Site 4, the author suggests that you do so before going on to the beaches to the south. A walk up the beach of a little more than 2/10 mile north brings you to the approximate center of East Beach. Turn to Site 4 and follow the descriptions. After visiting Site 4, return to this point and continue on to East End Beach, following the descriptions below.

EAST END BEACH

Cardinal

This beach extends from the Coast Guard Beach crossover through the beach in front of the King and Prince Hotel. The terra-cotta roofs of the King and Prince are visible about 1/2 mile to the south. The area just south of the crossover is the vicinity where Postell Creek once emptied into the ocean (see inlet site, Figure 20). Postell Creek separated East Beach from East End, making East Beach an island only accessible by bridge. Site 5 describes the landfilling of the inlet in the late 1920s, which fused together the two subdivisions and their beaches. Figure 21 shows that these two beaches have exhibited markedly different growth and erosion patterns for the past century. Today these two beaches still behave in much the same way as they did when they were separated by an inlet; East Beach continues to grow, while East End Beach undergoes alternating patterns of growth and erosion. This becomes evident as you compare the beaches to the north and to the south of the crossover.

Muhley Grass

The view of the land from the beach as you walk south of the Coast Guard property, allows you to appreciate the extent of accretion that has taken place in East End Beach since the 1950s. The old 1950s shoreline of East End follows the larger oaks and pines about 1/10 mile in back of this beach at the time this book is being written. Wood Avenue, which we shall visit later, runs just behind the old shoreline (see Wood Ave. in Figure 20).

Construction for most of the new condominiums and other dwellings you see in front of the old shoreline occurred in the middle 1980s, when the beach was at its most expanded state. Building on land recently accreted by a beach, which has had a history of intermittent erosion and accretion, is risky for both the beach and the buildings. It comes as no surprise, with the recent waxing and waning of this section of beach, that the condominium owners have already made application for seawall construction.

The first part of the Ocean Beach section tells how seawalls tend to cause the loss of beaches. Even though this section points out that there is ample sand moving with St. Simons' longshore currents, it is impossible to predict whether East End Beach would survive the new set of dynamics imposed by the seawalls. As Orrin Pilkey has oftentimes explained, beaches are placed in jeopardy to protect man-made structures. The above pattern of beachfront development has caused the loss of thousands of miles of America's beaches.[5]

BEACH RENOURISHMENT

Beach renourishment, which involves pumping dredge spoils onto a beach, is an alternative for combating beach erosion. Renourished beaches, with their sand mixed with silt and shells, are a poor substitute for natural sand beaches, both aesthetically and for support of wildlife. The fine silts occupy air spaces between the sand grains, smothering myriad tiny organisms (see psammon, page 22). This robs shorebirds and other animals of a valuable food source. The silty beaches often become sufficiently compact and hard as to prevent sea turtles from digging nests for their eggs for a year or more after renourishment.[13] If a natural beach does not remain in an area, then an artificial beach will not either. For this reason, groins and other holding structures are often required for beach renourishment.

Groins are walls that are constructed perpendicular to the shoreline (see Figure 23). Although groins may retain and even increase deposition of sand on the up-current side of the wall, they often cause erosion to beaches on the down-current side. As Figure 23 illustrates, groins interfere with the flow of the longshore currents along a beach, forcing the water to slow down as it goes around the rocks. This reduced speed and directional changes of the water flow causes suspended sand to drop out of the water on the up-current side of the groin. As the arrows indicate, some of the water is jetted off the tip of the groin, carrying some of the remaining sand into the deeper waters outside of the

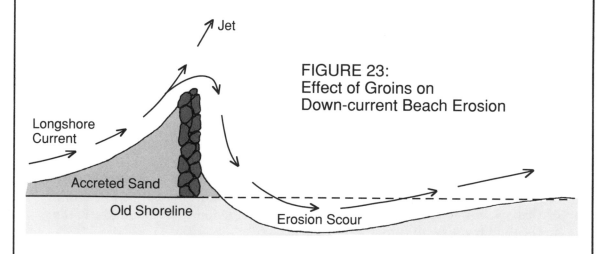

Jet

FIGURE 23:
Effect of Groins on
Down-current Beach Erosion

Longshore Current

Accreted Sand

Old Shoreline

Erosion Scour

longshore current; the longer the groin and/or the greater the speed of the current, the more sand is lost in this manner. The remaining water that comes around the groin has little sand left for the beaches on the other side. The churning of the water as it moves around the end of the groin creates eddy currents, which tend to scour away sand on the down-current side. These two effects are the major causes for the erosion of the down-current beaches. Depending on their length and the speed of the water current, groins can cause erosion to thousands of feet of shoreline on their down-current sides. By 1992 five states have banned groin construction because of damage they produce.

Beach renourishment may be a necessary alternative for some beaches, which are chronically eroding and have little or no natural sand reserves. Plans for beach renourishment which include groins have been proposed for the East End and St. Simons Beaches. As we have seen, there is an abundant reservoir of sand at Goulds Inlet and East Beach and the beaches in question alternately grow and erode. With the exorbitant costs and potential for destruction, the proposed beach renourishment programs for St. Simons Island so far have not been popular with a majority of the residents of Glynn County.

Amphipod

Return to your vehicles and drive to Wood Avenue, which is the first road to the left after exiting the Coast Guard Beach parking area. As you drive along this short length of road and look toward the beach, you are about one block in from the 1950s shoreline of East End Beach. The larger oaks and pines and the few older houses, originally fronting the beach, will help you discern the location of the old shoreline. From the road you can see the recent constructions in front of the old shoreline. More of East End Beach will be seen from Massengale Park and from the King and Prince Hotel, Sites 6 and 7, after visiting the East Beach Causeway, Site 5.

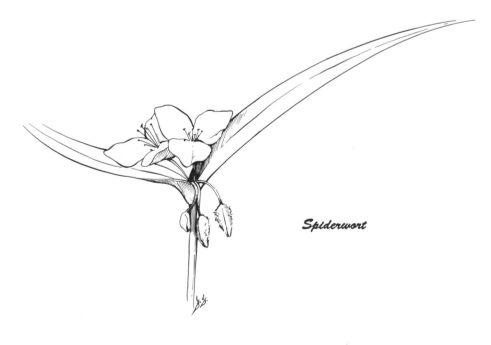

Spiderwort

Site #4: East Beach

Areas: East Beach and its accreted areas

The center of East Beach is about 2/10 mile north of the Coast Guard Beach crossover or about 1/2 mile south of Goulds Inlet Park, depending from which direction you are coming. As you walk along the center of East Beach, you can see that it is farther out to sea than the rest of St. Simons' beaches (see Figure 24). On a lower tide, you see the many associated shoals of East Beach extending more than 1/2 mile out to sea.

Most of the sand making up the shoals comes from southerly directed longshore currents, which bring sand from the barrier islands to the north. The massive shoals off East Beach build up where the southerly directed tidal flow, from Goulds Inlet, merges with the eastwardly directed discharge from St. Simons Sound, during ebb tide. Figure 24 depicts the ebb-tidal flow, coming from Goulds Inlet, moving over the submerged shoals at high tide. The turning arrows indicate where the two currents merge, slowing one another down and causing the suspended sand they are carrying to settle out and form shoals. Over the years the shoals have protected East Beach and have provided ample sand for its growth and the growth of the beaches to the south.

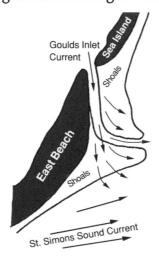

FIGURE 24: Merging of St. Simons and Goulds Inlet Ebb Tide Currents at a Higher Tide

The shape of East Beach constantly changes, in response to the shifting of the Goulds Inlet channels and the offshore shoals. Site 2 has more information on the shifting of Goulds Inlet's channels and the effects it has on the beaches.

In the center of East Beach, you should encounter a 1/2 acre pond, a short distance in back of the dunes. Prior to 1982, the back edge of the pond was the high-tide line of this part of East Beach. In the spring of that year, shoal ridges grew out from each end of this length of beach and joined, forming the pond and a new shoreline about 100 feet seaward. By the summer of 1986, the beach had accreted another 100 yards, leaving the pond nestled behind a field of sea oat-covered dunes, out of touch with the tide. The drawing on the opposite page depicts the above process. Over that time period, two smaller ponds were produced seaward of the larger pond. Since then, gradual erosion washed away the smaller ponds and brought the larger pond closer to the beach, so that today (1993) seawater occasionally overwashes into the pond during storms and highest tides.

Any of the many paths leading from the beach to the houses offers a view of the massive amount of land that has accreted over the years. An especially good view of the accreted land is seen from the third path north of the Coast Guard Beach crossover. The paths in this area are difficult to spot from the beach, because of their being overgrown by the wax myrtles, but this path is located near a solitary pine growing among the myrtles.

The path leads you through a small dune field and a shrub zone of wax myrtles to a clearing, which gives you a full view of the houses in back of the accreted land. Today a little more than 2/10 mile of dunes, meadows and shrubs lie between the houses and the beach. The original houses fronted the beach 60 years ago. The two relic dune ridges closest to you which cross the path are the same ones that were pointed out and dated near the Coast Guard Beach crossover in Site 3. The shrub forest, growing on the accreted land between you and the Coast Guard Beach parking area would also be growing here, if it were not for the periodic mowing this area receives.

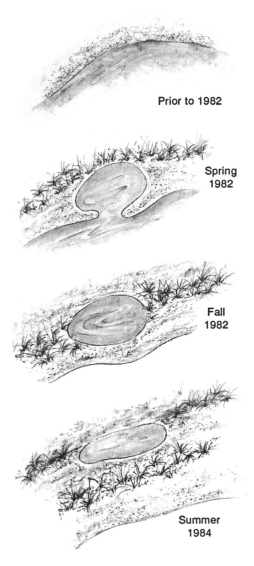

Prior to 1982

Spring 1982

Fall 1982

Summer 1984

East Beach pond

The wood planks, which you just walked over, bridge the southern extent of a slough that was formed in the early 1970s, when the beach was located here. The slough formed in much the same way as the first pond that we just saw. As the beach grew seaward, the pond narrowed and underwent the successive stages, to become the slough you see today. (See Freshwater Slough, page 35.) The slough runs parallel to the beach, in back of the wax myrtles, for a little over 1/10 mile. The water level of the slough varies greatly with rainfall and may dry up during draughts. Carolina willows, cattails and other wetland plants reveal the slough's presence, when the water is not there. The lighter green tops of the taller willows can be seen from the other side of the myrtle bushes, giving you a way of locating the slough from the beach. As we have seen, this part of East Beach has had a history of saltatory growth, leaving ponds behind in the process.

Site#5: East Beach Causeway

Areas: The marsh between the islands of East Beach,
East End and St. Simons Island

East Beach Causeway is a 1/2-mile road that runs from Demere Road to the Coast Guard Station. Find an area on the causeway reasonably close to Postell Creek bridge and park where there is sufficient shoulder on the opposite side from the bike path. Position youself so that you have a clear view of the marsh on both sides. A quick review of the Geology section, pages 11 through 15, will be helpful in the understanding of content of the next paragraph.

Looking west toward Demere Road, you see the ancient (Pleistocene) shore-line of St. Simons Island bordering the marsh. Looking toward the northeast, you can see in the distance how Sea Island and East Beach align (see Figure 19). Most of the island residents consider East Beach and East End to be integral parts of St. Simons Island. But it is clear, from what we see here and understand from the Geology section, that they are Holocene formations, similar to Sea Island. And, they were formed during a different geological time period than was St. Simons Island.

The broadening of the marsh to the north and its narrowing to the south show the difference in the orientations of the Holocene and Pleistocene shorelines. On the south side of the causeway, the marsh comes to an abrupt end, where the Holocene and Pleistocene Islands merged in the area of Arnold Road (see Figure 19). As you traverse either the East Beach or the Sea Island causeway, consider that an entire ice age, of approximately 35,000 years, took place from the time the ocean washed the shores of St. Simons Island, until the time of the formation of Sea Island, East End and East Beach. Sites 12 and 15 and the Sea Island Causeway offer views of Sea Island from St. Simons' shores, from more northern locations.

Stand on the little bridge over Postell Creek and look toward the Coast Guard Station. Prior to 1926, Postell Creek, which drained the marsh on both sides of the present causeway, coursed across the land just south of the Coast Guard Station and emptied into the ocean, whose shoreline at that time was close to the other side of the station. (See inlet site in Figure 20.) This made East Beach a separate island, only accessible by a bridge from East End (the East Beach causeway did not exist at that time).

In 1926 and again in 1928, the inlet and most of the associated wetlands were landfilled, connecting East Beach and East End. Today, pockets of marsh and standing tidal water are on the other side of Ocean Boulevard. These and wetlands, identifiable by the Carolina willows on the beach side of Wood Avenue, mark the approximate pathway made by Postell Creek to the ocean 64 years ago.

The water running in Postell Creek appears "dirty" and may even look polluted. This appearance is due to the sediments and abundant life suspended in the tidal water. The Salt Marsh section, pages 31 and 32, discusses the importance of the organisms in these gray-brown marsh waters as a life-support system for the great oceans.

The slimy, gold-colored areas on the mud creek banks are a type of sessile diatom (algae) which comes in with the tide and, as the name implies, attaches itself to mud, sand, cordgrass stalks and other objects inundated by the tide. These diatoms are a valuable food source for fiddler crabs and other small animals in and surrounding the marsh creeks.

At a lower tide, you may see fiddler crabs close to their burrows in the creek banks, near and under the bridge. If you remain fairly still and quiet, you may see a male waving his large claw, with which he tries to attract a female to his burrow to breed.

Sand Fiddler

Also at a lower tide, this bridge is one of the best locations for seeing the secretive clapper rails, whose "laughing" calls are often heard, but the bird rarely seen. The clapper rail is an inconspicuous, slender, pigeon-sized, gray-brown bird. It stalks along the creek banks, probing the mud for burrowing animals with its long beak. Its upturned tail and deliberate, chicken-like gait earns for the bird the fitting name of marsh hen.

Clapper Rail

*Willets during
courtship display*

From the southern shoulder of the causeway, you see that most of the marsh near the shoulder is salt pan.   As you travel the different causeways, you frequently find salt pans in the marsh areas bordering roads, because roadbeds often cut off much of the marsh's tidal circulation. (The Salt Marsh section, page 27, describes salt pans and their origins.) The hard-packed sand of the salt pans provides less wet walking conditions for exploring the marsh. The marsh may be entered at any point along the causeway.

During the warmer seasons, large numbers of sand fiddlers are often seen on the salt pans, foraging on the sessile diatoms, other algae and detritus (dead organic matter) left behind by the tide. Sand fiddlers are recognized by their large white claws and purple color on their backs. Most of the zonal plant communities described in the Salt Marsh section are seen surrounding these hammocks. Many of the hammocks show different degrees of development, as seen by the vegetation they support.

When walking the sandy paths between the hammocks toward the south, the marsh becomes wetter and the cordgrass taller, as you approach a small tributary of Postell Creek. Listen for the metallic, house wren-like songs of the long-billed marsh wrens, who inhabit the tall cordgrass near the creek banks.

The darker fiddler crabs, with the yellow claws, crawling about on the mud, among the taller cordgrass stalks, are mud fiddlers. Keep your eyes peeled for a super-large fiddler (almost twice the size of a mud fiddler), having a large white claw with red dots at the joints. This is the rarer-seen, brackish-water fiddler (mentioned in the Salt Marsh section, page 29).

If you hear a frantic, repeating call, "will-will-willet," look up in the direction of the sound, to see the male willet displaying his beautiful black and white-striped wings, while hovering in the air. This striking mating display is a common sight over the marshes in the spring and early summer.

Site #6 Massengale Park

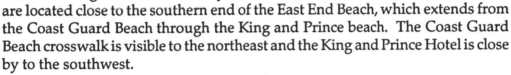

Areas: Old shorelines and forests of the southern part of East End Beach

Massengale Park is on Ocean Boulevard, about 4/10 mile south of East Beach Causeway. Park your vehicle in the Massengale lot and walk to the beach. Figure 19 shows that you are located close to the southern end of the East End Beach, which extends from the Coast Guard Beach through the King and Prince beach. The Coast Guard Beach crosswalk is visible to the northeast and the King and Prince Hotel is close by to the southwest.

Historically, the beaches from the presently undeveloped property, just north of Massengale to the King and Prince, have exhibited the least amount of growth of the East End Beaches. In 1986, when the growth in East End and East Beach were at their greatest extents, one only had to walk about 150 feet to reach the high tide line from the Massengale parking lot. Since the fall of 1986, the beach has retreated to one-third that distance. The crosswalk that spans the narrow area of dry beach and a rock seawall which extends from Massengale Park through the Sea Island tract to the north has just been built at the time of writing this guide.

After exploring the beach, walk toward the park pavilion. As you approach the pavilion, you come upon a small grassed sand ridge which crosses the park grounds. This is all that remains of the old 1950s shoreline. After years of foot traffic and grounds maintenance, it is a wonder that it still exists.

Looking at the oaks near the pavilion, you see that the trees closest to the ocean are small and appear slanted away from the direction of the sea breezes. Winds, carrying salt spray from the ocean, dehydrate and often kill exposed buds and leaves, which stunt the growth of the trees. The windward limbs become more stunted than those on the protected leeward sides. This differential "salt pruning" causes the trees to grow in this characteristic lopsided manner. This is contrary to the common misconception that the trees are stooped over by the force of the prevailing winds. Whole forests fronting the ocean often assume backward-slanting canopies called shear lines, because they have the appearance of being trimmed with hedge clippers (see Figure 25).

Notice that the limbs on the windward side of Massengale's oaks tend to be bushier than those on the leeward side. The terminal bud at the end of a limb normally inhibits the growth of the lateral buds on the young stem (see tree limb

Wind

FIGURE 25:
Trees Shorn by Ocean Breezes and Salt Spray

illustrations below). The terminal bud, being at the tip of the stem, is usually the first bud to be killed by the dessicating winds and salt. Death of the terminal bud prematurely releases growth of the lateral buds, giving the limb many lateral branches, as the illustration portrays. Each lateral branch has its own terminal and lateral buds and many of these are affected in the same way. By this process the wind-exposed trees become many-branched and shrubby. This same effect is achieved when bushes around the house are regularly trimmed.

Notice that older live oaks throughout this area and East Beach tend to be smaller and have more branches than those in the more protected areas of the island. The expansive forests, which extend from the beaches to the western-facing marshes on Jekyll Island, graphically show these differences in tree development and the other above-described features, as you travel the roads that circle the island.

Terminal Bud

Lateral
Bud

Intact branch

The trees of Massengale Park and adjacent lots are the only remains of the true Holocene maritime forest of East End. The older live oaks and pines, scattered among the homes of East Beach, are a remnant of East Beach's Holocene forest. The soils of these younger island forests are poorer and support a lower diversity of tree species, than those of the older Pleistocene island of St. Simons, as we shall see on Site 11.

Growth of lateral buds
after loss of terminal bud

Leaving the entrance of the park, you see the southern extreme of Bloody Marsh on the other side of Ocean Boulevard. The point where East End, when it was an island, joined onto St. Simons Island is in the vicinity of Arnold Road, at the blinking light to the left. Site 5 describes the merging of the two islands to produce the land features that you are seeing here. East Beach Causeway appears to the right where the cars are crossing the marsh in the distance.

To drive to Site 7, turn left onto Ocean Boulevard. Again turn left at the blinking light, onto Arnold Road. Find a place to park, near the King and Prince Hotel.

Site #7: King and Prince

Area: The beach in front of the King and Prince Hotel

The King and Prince seawall is the southern extreme of East End Beach, and extends farther seaward than any other feature along that stretch of shoreline. The seawall has protected the hotel from the many storms that have eroded the neighboring beaches, since it was erected by the Navy during the second World War. Over the years this has accentuated the seaward extension of the wall and the hotel, which allows the King and Prince's terra cotta roofs to be visible from so many areas of St. Simons' beaches.

During the 1950s erosion, eight vertical feet of the King and Prince seawall was exposed and seawater was reaching around the wall, into the hotel grounds on the north side. Another concrete seawall was then constructed, to the north of the Navy-built wall, to block further erosion on that side.

It wasn't until the late 1960s that sand began to accumulate in front of the King and Prince seawalls. This happened several years after the rest of the East End beaches had accreted more than 100 feet of dry sand in front of their 1950 shoreline. Sand accretion on this beach was (and still is) retarded by its extreme seaward position and because of the inhibitory effects of seawalls on beach growth. (The Ocean Beach section, page 20, describes the effect of seawalls on beach growth.) By 1986 over 100 feet of sea oat-covered dunes and beach had accumulated in front of the hotel seawall.

Joining the ranks of other East End property owners, the King and Prince took advantage of the recent accretionary growth and erected their North Villas in 1985. In the process they tore down the wall that protected the north end of the property, to make more room for the condominiums. With the recent erosion of the shoreline, the high-tide line came within 30 feet of the property line of the North Villas by the summer of 1991. This necessitated the building of a rip-rap (rock) seawall in front of the Villas, which has since been extended in front of the old Navy-built wall. How this seaward extension of the new wall will affect future accretion on this already fragile beach is unpredictable.

Site #8: St. Simons Beach

Area: The beach between the King and Prince and the fishing pier

Figure 20 shows the location of St. Simons Beach. This beach had a history of erosion, before the placement of the Johnson Rocks in 1964. Since then, the beach shows minor fluctuations of growth and erosion, which at best only produces a moderate-sized beach. South of the King and Prince, St. Simons' beaches diminish progressively as they come closer to the fast-moving tidal flow, that runs through the inlet of St. Simons Sound. (See Detail of Figure 19 on the opposite page.) Since these beaches are under more of the influence of the tidal currents, let us take a closer look at the forces that affect the tidal flow in this area.

The greatest contributor to the ebb-tide flow through the inlet is the Brunswick River. The flow from the Brunswick River courses along the 40-foot-deep Brunswick Ship Channel, which deflects off the northern end of Jekyll Island and runs across the inlet toward St. Simons Island. The force of this tidal flow is fueled by the additional flow from the McKay, Frederica and Back Rivers. The main current swings wide of the curving ship channel and strikes St. Simons island just east of the fishing pier, scouring much of St. Simons Beach and the pier area (see Detail of Figure 19). A natural 80-foot-deep scour hole, close to the beach in front of the lighthouse, is a testimony to the speed and volume of water that moves through this area.

The direction of the tidal flow out to sea is revealed by the channel shoals, which are visible at a lower tide, from most of St. Simons and East End beaches. The shoals emerge close to the Seventh and Eighth Street section of St. Simons Beach and go off in a northeasterly direction, as the island's shoreline curves to the north (see Figure 19). Channel shoals are created in places where fast-flowing deeper water shears against slower-moving water closer to the land. The friction created by the shearing slows the faster-moving water, causing some of its suspended sand to fall out, which forms the finger-like shoals. The channel shoals and the above-mentioned currents in St. Simons Sound and Inlet can be seen to advantage from the top of the lighthouse, Site 9.

During the "early resort days," 1880s to 1920s, visitors coming off the ferry at the Village pier were carried by a horse-drawn trolley to the large and famous Hotel St. Simons, which was then located on the Massengale tract.[8] Beachview Drive, which begins at Mallory Street in the Village and ends behind the King and

Prince Hotel, was a major part of the old trolley bed and was then called Railroad Avenue. Postell Avenue ran parallel to Beachview Drive, one block closer to the beach. Up to the 1930s, beachfront houses on 150-foot-deep lots backed up to Postell Avenue. The lots between Postell and Beachview were also 150 feet deep (see Figure 26).

Since the 1930s, storms have steadily eroded this section of beach, first cutting through Postell Avenue and eventually through Beachview. In the fall of 1964, Hurricane Dora washed out some houses between Sixth and Seventh Streets, leaving this shoreline in its most-retreated position. Figure 26 outlines the total area eroded from 1926 to just after Hurricane Dora. In 1964 President Lyndon Johnson ordered the erection of the rip-rap seawall known as the "Johnson Rocks".

Today this section of the Johnson Rocks armors the beaches from south of the King and Prince property to about 1/2 mile west of the fishing pier (see Figure 20). Since the emplacement of this section of the wall, all landward erosion in this area has been halted. The other section of the Johnson Rocks is located on the Goulds Inlet and upper East Beach areas, mentioned in Site 2.

A remaining, half-block fragment of Postell Avenue is seen opposite the entrance of the historic lighthouse-keeper's house on Twelfth Street. Walking up this segment of Postell Avenue, you can see the angle that the road took as it went toward the King and Prince area. The two houses and a sun deck that you see to the right, now sandwiched between that segment of road and the seawall, are all that remains of the once-large beachfront residential area south of Postell Avenue.

Detail of FIGURE 19

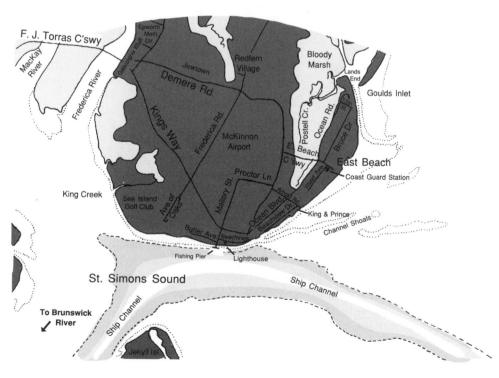

Another fragment of Postell Avenue is the one-block-long road connecting the ends of Cedar and Myrtle Streets near the seawall, immediately south of King and Prince property (see Figure 26). This fragment of Postell and the accompanying lots owe their existence to an old seawall seen behind the Johnson Rocks, that was built prior to the devastating erosion of the 1950s.

The northern segment of Beachview Drive borders the back of the King and Prince property, by the tennis courts, and runs south to where it ends at Fifth Street. The Fifth Street end of Beachview gives you an excellent view of the eroded shoreline to the south. The other segment of Beachview goes east from Mallory Street in the Village to the blinking traffic light where Ocean Boulevard and Demere Road intersect (see Figure 26). Between Twelfth Street and Oglethorpe Avenue, Beachview Drive curves sharply to the left. At the curve, the remaining fragment of the original Beachview Drive (Railroad Avenue) continues straight, as a short dirt road with a cottage on both sides, ending in a seawall. This area now serves as a public access to the beach.

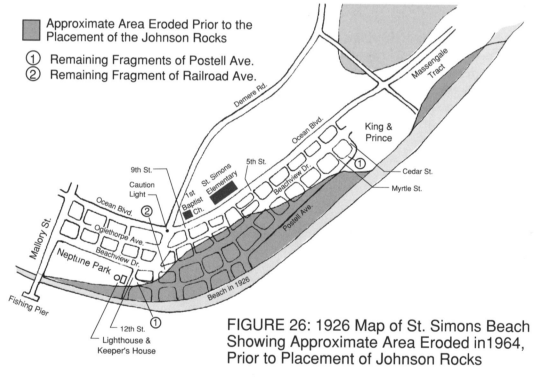

FIGURE 26: 1926 Map of St. Simons Beach Showing Approximate Area Eroded in 1964, Prior to Placement of Johnson Rocks

A view of the entire eroded section, between the two segments of Beachview, can be seen on the beach at the Ninth Street beach access, which is opposite the First Baptist Church on Ocean Boulevard. From this vantage point you see the entire 500-to 600-foot-deep section of developed land that was claimed by the ocean over the years, prior to the placement of the Johnson Rocks. On the beach just south of the Ninth Street access are the remains of an artesian well that was in the backyard of one of the houses lining Beachview Drive, when it existed in this area. Its presence is often given away by birds drinking or children playing in the fresh water gurgling out of the sand.

Site # 9: The Fishing Pier and St. Simons Sound Beach

Areas: The beaches near the fishing pier and west along St. Simons Sound and the view from the top of the St. Simons Lighthouse.

The beaches in the vicinity of the fishing pier and those to the west have undergone a more gradual erosion over the years than St. Simons Beach. In the 1920s the beach in the pier area extended out to about where the wings of the fishing pier occur today. The old pier extended at least the length of the present pier out from that shore. Oldtimers remember when they could drive their cars on the beach from King Creek, near the Sea Island Golf Club, to the beach in front of the present-day Coast Guard Station, in the 1920s. If it were not for the Postell Creek Inlet, separating East Beach from the rest of St. Simons Island (Figure 20), they could have continued all the way to Goulds Inlet.

Since the early 1930s, these beaches had been steadily retreating until the placement of the Johnson Rocks in 1964. Since then, the seawall has so far prevented further landward retreat, but some loss of beach elevation has occurred. From the fishing pier, you can recognize how high the tide rises by the dark discoloration on the rocks. If the seawall were not here, the beach would be well on its way back toward the brick county buildings, back of Neptune Park.

The beach west of the fishing pier is known as the St. Simons Sound Beach (see Figure 20). From the end of the fishing pier you have a good view of the sound shoreline. You see that the Johnson Rocks end about a half-mile to the west of the pier, fairly close to a pine-covered headland, which juts out from the shoreline. In that area you can see that the sandy beach becomes a marsh. King Creek is about another 1/2 mile on the other side (west) of the headland.

If the tide is sufficiently low, you can see from the pier massive, sandy-mud tidal flats that extend from the sound beaches. During the lowest point in the tide cycle, the glistening tidal flats extend even farther out into the inlet than the fishing pier. The fast-moving ebb-tidal currents coming from the Frederica, MacKay and Back Rivers swing away from St. Simons Sound Beach, as they come around the southwestern end of the island (see Detail of Figure 19). Being on the inside of the turn, waters near this section of beach move slower, allowing much of the suspended mud and fine sand to fall out to form the tidal flat. (The reasons for deposition under these circumstances is described in the Salt Marsh section on meandering, page 29.) The outflow from the three rivers merge with the tidal discharge from the Brunswick River and head out through the St. Simons Inlet.

Although periodic erosion and accretion occur in various places, a sandy beach has persisted throughout the years along the southwestern section of St. Simons Sound shoreline. In the early 1980s, the Sea Island Company built a seawall which skirted St. Simons Sound Beach, from the area near the end of the Johnson Rocks to the west side of the headland, to prevent further erosion of their golf club grounds. Since then, most of the beach in that southwestern section has disappeared and has been replaced by marsh. Presently this area continues to undergo rapid change.

Closer to the pier, about 3/10 mile to the west, a small outcropping of naturally formed rock is visible in the middle of the beach at a lower tide. In lieu of walking or biking down the beach to get a closer look at the rock and the beach areas beyond, you can drive down Butler Avenue to Hamilton Street (see map, Detail of Figure 19). Turn left onto HamiltonStreet and park at the public beach access at the end of the street. You should see the rock outcropping at middle to low tide as you cross the boardwalk to the beach.

The porous rock consists of the mineral humate and is often referred to as "bog iron." Humate is formed by the chemical binding of iron salts with the humus or organic matter in marsh soils. Through the action of bacteria in the clay and dissolved oxygen in the water, the iron salts (principally iron sulfide) become oxidized, to form a low-grade iron ore (iron oxide). In this case, the resulting iron ore, humate, is in the form of a dark reddish-black crumbly rock, harboring eroded pits and impressions where plants and animals occupied the clay. The presence of "bog iron" is evidence that this area was once a salt marsh.

Since the dynamic shoreline near the headland is only 2/10 mile west of Hamilton Street, you may want to have a closer look at this interesting area. Because this beach was undergoing rapid changes during the writing of this guide, you may well discover further changes.

THE LIGHTHOUSE

The fantastic view from the top of the lighthouse is well worth the climb up the 129 steps. From its top you can see the entire shoreline from Goulds Inlet to the marsh beaches of St. Simons Sound. The panoramic view allows you to see that the beach virtually wraps around the bottom of the island, giving you an appreciation of why its different sections respond differently to daily tides, winds and weather conditions.

People who have flown over the Georgia coast are often surprised by the density of the live oak canopy which covers St. Simons and the other barrier islands. The lighthouse is just high enough to see above the canopy. Notice how much taller the pines rise above the live oak canopy. The Maritime Forest section mentions the little tolerance that pines have for shade, so height is their way of dealing with competition for sunlight in a fully developed maritime forest.

When the wind is not appreciably disturbing the water, lines of white foam can be seen outlining the areas of the faster-moving water. The friction generated between bodies of water moving at different speeds causes little circular currents (eddy currents), where the waters shear against one another. The little eddy currents whip the water into a froth, creating streaks of foam along the shear lines. Depending on the wind and tide, parallel foam lines often outline areas of the ship channel. The tidal currents from the Frederica, McKay and Back Rivers are often outlined in foam, as they swing wide around the southwestern end of the island. The edges of the tidal currents which swing close to the pier and move along St. Simons Beach are often delineated by foam. At a lower tide, the channel shoals mentioned in Site 8 are visible. The paired buoys, marking the entrance of the ship channel, can be seen to the southeast. While at the lighthouse, see the exhibits and the collection of books on the island's history at the Museum of Coastal History.

Site #10: Bloody Marsh Monument

Areas: St. Simons Island shoreline, Bloody Marsh, and the marsh side of East Beach

The entrance to the monument is on Demere Road about 1/2 mile north of the East Beach causeway (see Figure 19). The parking area is surrounded by live oaks, which show the gnarled, more-than-usual branching, typical of oaks assaulted by sea breezes. A slanting, shear line on the canopy of the trees growing close to this shoreline is clearly seen from the granite monument looking across the marsh toward the ocean. A explanation for these wind-induced growth features is found in Site 6.

You are standing on the ancient shoreline of St. Simons Island, which was a beach 35,000 years ago, before the formation of East Beach and Sea Island. The land you see, directly across the marsh, is East Beach and the causeway to East Beach is seen to the south. The open area just north of East Beach is Goulds Inlet, which separates East Beach from Sea Island. The terra-cotta roofs of The Cloister, Sea Island's resort hotel, are visible in the distance.

The marsh adjacent to the park is high and sandy and can be walked on at a lower tide. Typical of a high marsh, there are salt pans with glasswort, saltwort and salt grass communities. Needle rush hammocks are close to the park's grass banks. If the tide and temperature conditions are right, you may encounter herds of foraging sand fiddlers scurrying over the salt pans. Clear zonation is seen from the marsh to the mainland, starting with needle rush and sea oxeye at the marsh border, and groundsel trees and marsh elder at the edge of the marsh. By its position just above the upper level of the tidal range, it is easy to appreciate why marsh elder is often called high tide bush. Cedars occupy a transition zone just above the marsh edge, and finally, the live oaks dominate the upland. (The Salt Marsh, page 26, illustrates marsh zonation.)

Bunch grass (*Spartina bakeri*), a rarer relative of the smooth cordgrass (*Spartina alterniflora*) and salt meadow cordgrass (*Spartina patens*), is seen at the edge of the bank near the granite monument. Bunch grass appears like a taller version of salt meadow hay and grows in definite clumps, deserving of its name. It occurs in areas where there is frequent fresh water runoff, as is the case here, and is a principal plant in fresh water marshes.

Site #11: Mid-island Forests

Area: The mid-island forests seen from Frederica and Lawrence Roads

Most of the trees that you see on Frederica and Lawrence Roads are younger than 100 years. Prior to the turn of the century most of the land along the center of the island was cotton fields. The island had been sufficiently deforested that James Gould's grandparents recall looking, from their porch, across cotton fields at boats sailing by Sea Island.[14] Their house is located on the west side of Frederica Road, just north of the Lord of Life Lutheran Church.

Most of the trees along Frederica Road are live oak and pines mixed with pignut hickory, laurel oak, water oak and sweet gum. These are typical of forest communities on older barrier islands. The soils of the older (Pleistocene) islands are more mature and support a greater variety of tree species, than those of younger (Holocene) islands, such as East Beach, Site 6. The large stretch of undeveloped land along Lawrence Road (above the Christ Church turnoff) supports dense stands of visibly younger trees. This area was one of the last large areas to be farmed on St. Simons Island.

Hackberry

Site #12: Harrington

Areas: The community along South Harrington Road and the marsh between St. Simons and Sea Islands

South Harrington Road is 1.6 miles north of the traffic light at the intersection of Frederica and Sea Island Roads. After passing Bennie's Red Barn restaurant, make a right turn onto South Harrington Road. As you travel along South Harrington, the old live oaks, owner-made homes and overgrown lots leave you with a sense of rustic timelessness. This is the settlement of Harrington, where black families have owned these properties since they were given to slaves after the Civil War. Harrington has been spared being bought up and developed, because many of the properties are "heir deeded" or passed down from generation to generation, making clear title impossible. Jewtown and Proctor Lane are two other black settlements on St. Simons Island that have much the same history.

In little over 1/2 mile, South Harrington Road becomes a diked road, which runs through the marsh to Harrington Landing, now called Village Creek Landing, which was a loading dock for Little St. Simons Island. Recently the dock facilities have become a fish camp which is opened to the public. The porch and bay windows of the upstairs snack bar offer an outstanding panoramic view of the back side of Sea Island, south side of Little St. Simons Island, and the old shoreline of St. Simons Island with the marshes between. Figures 19 and 1 should help orient you to what you are seeing from this view.

This site takes you far enough into the marsh, so you can watch terns and ospreys working the water, a great egret poised in total stillness awaiting a hapless fish, mullet and menhaden prickling the water surface as they flee a predator, and the fluid movements of an otter occasioning nearby. In the quietness of this place you can hear oysters popping and muffled bird calls among the reeds. You can also hear fish jumping, insects buzzing and other busy sounds of life blended in with wind, gently rustling the cordgrass.

Site #13: The Live Oaks of Christ Church

Areas: Christ Church, natural history and uses of live oaks and the swamp forest of woodland walk.

Christ Church is three miles north of the traffic light at the intersection of Frederica and Sea Island Roads. Be sure to follow Frederica Road to the left at the fork, as signs to Christ Church and Ft. Frederica indicate. This section of Frederica Road, which includes Christ Church and Fort Frederica, has the oldest and most beautiful live oaks on the island. Just before reaching Christ Church, Frederica Road cuts through brackish wetlands, which are an extension of the Dunbar tidal creek system mentioned in Site 16.

The setting of Christ Church dates back to the colonial days. Its amazing history is described in most of the historical references in Appendix D and on the signs and gravestones on site. What is indescribable, however, is the sublime setting of the church, which nests with understated elegance under a canopy of massive live oaks. Many have tried to capture this sublime setting on canvas and film.

LIVE OAKS

An old adage says that live oaks take a hundred years to grow, a hundred years to live and a hundred years to die. Live oaks reach their largest size between 200 and 300 years. Because of their stout, gnarled trunks and great twisting boughs, most people overestimate the age of live oaks. They grow faster than people realize. Edwin Stephens, who studied the growth of live oaks in Louisiana, said that a 30-year-old live oak may have a trunk two feet in diameter and most 100-year-old live oaks average trunk diameters of 5.5 feet.[15] The live oaks that line the driveway to the Sea Island Golf Club (Avenue of the Oaks) were planted in 1848-49, making them close to 150 years old (see Figure 19).[8]

There is no record of the age of the oaks surrounding Christ Church. Through estimations made from old photographs and drawings, from size comparisons and from limb loss, most of the Christ Church trees appear to be well over 200 years old and in the descending third of their life span. The largest live oak in Georgia is 86 feet high, with a trunk diameter of 10 feet. Its 143-foot-wide crown shades close to 1/2 acre of ground. This giant is located in Baptist Village, Waycross.[16]

Growth patterns and sizes of live oaks vary with exposure to wind, sun, salt spray and quality of soil. The oaks at Christ Church and Ft. Frederica are fairly well protected from wind and are growing in good soil conditions. Compare these to the smaller, bushier live oaks, exposed to the ocean breezes and poorer soils of the younger island formations of Massengale Park, Site 6.

The word "live" describes the fact that this species appears to retain its leaves throughout most of the year. Actually, live oaks drop their leaves as new ones emerge. Residents living under live oaks are painfully aware that each oak appears to have its own time for dropping its leaves, from October through April, making leaf raking a never-ending job.

Resurrection Fern

Lichen

Spanish Moss

Live oaks, *Quercus virginiana*, are confined mostly to the coastal plain areas of the Southeastern Atlantic and Gulf states, from southern Virginia through eastern Texas and some occur on the west coast of Cuba.[16] Most live oaks grow in poor sandy soils. To help cope with the dry, nutrient-poor conditions, live oaks, similar to other coastal plants, have shallow, spreading root systems. In maritime forests the root systems of trees and understory plants interlock, supporting one another in strong winds. Without their companions, single live oaks are susceptible to falling over in high winds and offer little resistance to a bulldozer.

Notice the resurrection fern growing on the trunks of the live oaks. This epiphytic fern, as the name implies, grows on

Lichens

the trunks of trees, drawing its nutrients from the decaying bark and materials that get trapped in the fern's furry fronds. The name resurrection refers to the way its leaves turn brown and curl during drought periods between rains, and with the next rainfall, "resurrect" as their leaves unfurl and again turn green. Tree bark does not hold water well and rains in the coastal area often are erratic, with periods of drought between. The abundance of resurrection fern all over the island testifies to the success of this fern's adaptation.

The great boughs of the live oaks also support a veritable vegetable garden of many kinds of lichens, bromeliads (air plants) and the rare green fly orchid (*Epidendrum conopseum*). Spanish moss is the most common of the four species of bromeliads that are found in coastal Georgia. A common misconception that Spanish moss is parasitic to trees is largely supported by a tendency for the plants to be present in large clumps on the dead tree limbs. Dead limbs simply offer the Spanish moss better access to sunlight, without the competition of leaves. (Site 14 has more information on Spanish moss.)

Lichens are a composite of a fungus and algae, which grow together in a mutually beneficial relationship. The fungus provides a protective housing, water and nutrients for itself and the algae living within its cells. The algae supplies food, through photosynthesis, for both plants. Most lichens are blue-green, due to the color of the algae's chlorophyll. A curious red-colored lichen, not as frequently seen as the blue-green, is pigmented by red fruiting bodies of the host fungus, *Haematomma* sp. The genus name is adopted from a medical term, hematoma, describing bleeding under the skin. Locals sometimes call it bubble gum lichen.

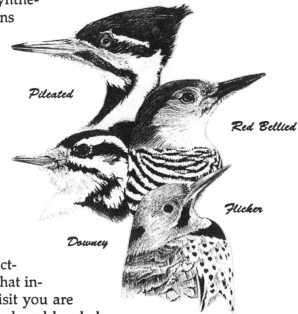

Pileated

Red Bellied

Flicker

Downey

Woodpeckers abound, attracted by the multitude of insects that inhabit these old trees. In one visit you are likely to see pileated, red-bellied, red-headed, hairy and downy woodpeckers, flickers and yellow-bellied sapsuckers.

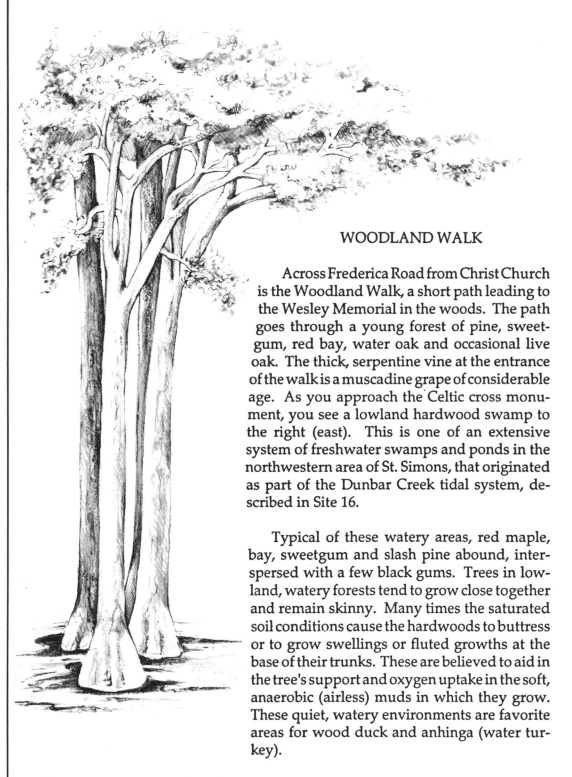

WOODLAND WALK

Across Frederica Road from Christ Church is the Woodland Walk, a short path leading to the Wesley Memorial in the woods. The path goes through a young forest of pine, sweetgum, red bay, water oak and occasional live oak. The thick, serpentine vine at the entrance of the walk is a muscadine grape of considerable age. As you approach the Celtic cross monument, you see a lowland hardwood swamp to the right (east). This is one of an extensive system of freshwater swamps and ponds in the northwestern area of St. Simons, that originated as part of the Dunbar Creek tidal system, described in Site 16.

Typical of these watery areas, red maple, bay, sweetgum and slash pine abound, interspersed with a few black gums. Trees in lowland, watery forests tend to grow close together and remain skinny. Many times the saturated soil conditions cause the hardwoods to buttress or to grow swellings or fluted growths at the base of their trunks. These are believed to aid in the tree's support and oxygen uptake in the soft, anaerobic (airless) muds in which they grow. These quiet, watery environments are favorite areas for wood duck and anhinga (water turkey).

OF MEN AND LIVE OAKS

The live oak's dense heavy wood, with its many curves and twisted grain, severely limits its use as lumber today. Before metal-hulled ships, these very same properties, coupled with the wood's resistance to rotting and weathering, made live oak the world's most sought-after lumber for shipbuilding from the mid-eighteenth to the mid-nineteenth centuries.

Jack Coggins in his book, *Ships and Seamen of the American Revolution*, describes how trees whose great limbs took on the desired curves of various boat parts were carefully chosen and cut into large pieces. They were sent to shipbuilders, where they were fashioned into massive frames (ribs), bow stems, keels, knees and other areas of the ship, where curves and strength were required. The accompanying illustration diagrams how some of the boat parts were hewn from different parts of a tree. As you can see from the illustration, the wood grain moves with the curves of the boat parts, thus preventing their snapping in two, due to splitting along the grain. The grain of live oak spirals and twists, which further maximizes strength, and which made live oak vessels superior warships.

Reports that British cannonballs bounced off the hull of the U.S.S. Constitution, a live oak ship during the war of 1812, gave it the name of "Old Ironsides." Live oak is so tough that shipwrights had to sharpen their cutting tools every 30 minutes, when hewing the oak while the wood was green. Cured live oak was simply too tough to cut.[17] One of the rangers at Ft. Frederica recalls that a log, from a live oak tree that had been dead for a long time, jammed a large pneumatic log splitter.

The demand for live oak for shipbuilding, in the United States and for export, was great and "live oaking" became a big business. Since it took from 400 to 700 live oaks to build the frame of one of these great sailing ships, many of our coastal and barrier island forests quickly disappeared. The live oak trade rapidly diminished in the middle 1800s, with the increased difficulty in procuring live oak and with the inception of "ironclad," steam-powered ships.[18] Beyond shipbuilding, there was limited use for such devilishly hard, heavy, curvaceous wood. Live oak was used for cannon carriages, wheel hubs and heavy wood supports, like some of those used in the construction of the Brooklyn Bridge in 1886.

Many of the trees, not taken for ship timbers, were cut down to clear land for cotton plantations in the late 1700s to middle 1800s. Few trees on St. Simons survived this onslaught, so most of the live oaks on the Island are not more than 100 years old. Today development of homes, condominiums, office complexes, shopping malls, and road widening continue to take live oaks. However, there is a growing public awareness of the beauty of live oaks and a greater intolerance towards their destruction. We are finally responding to the honor of having the live oak as Georgia's State Tree.

Site # 14: Ft. Frederica

Area: Ft. Frederica National Monument

The entrance to Ft. Frederica is less than a quarter mile west of Christ Church on Frederica Road.

The educational displays and movie at the interpretive center effectively portray the life of the people in this colonial military village and fort in 1742. The center has an excellent selection of regional nature and historical books. From the interpretive center, this guide follows one of the routes commonly taken by the tour guides, pointing out natural phenomena as you visit the historic displays and ruins.

The first part of our walk takes us to Broad Street, which leads from the interpretive center to the fort on the Frederica River. During the early spring, clusters of a saprophytic orchid, called coral root (*Corallorhiza wisteriana*), grow under the live oaks near the path leading from the interpretive center to the village grounds. The orchid is mud-colored, with a spike of small inconspicuous flowers, each with a purple-and-white spotted tongue-like lip (see illustration on opposite page). The orchid lacks leaves because it lives off of decaying plant matter, hence the name saprophyte. A boardwalk crosses over a giant muscadine grape vine, estimated to be over 200 years old.

The village site before you was founded on an Indian cornfield kept cleared by the British. The site was farmed, prior to its donation to the National Park Service by the Ft. Frederica Association in 1936. This is why most of the village site is clear of large trees. Two exceptions are an unusually large hackberry tree near the path, identified by its pale-colored leaves and prickly bark and a 250-year-old live oak, behind the ruin of Captain James MacKay's house (fifth sign on the left). Notice the large size of the live oak and the lightning damage on its western side.

During the first two to three weeks in May, Ladies' tresses (*Spiranthes* sp.), a ground-dwelling orchid commonly seen on the roadsides, grows near the MacKay live oak tree. As the scientific name implies, the many tiny white orchid flowers grow in an unusual spiral arrangement, on a one-foot-high spike (see illustration below). If you see ladies' tresses in bloom, then look for the tiny green three-petaled flower of the Spanish moss, which blooms at about the same time of year. The presence of the flower and a small slender seed pod are the evidence that Spanish moss is a flowering plant (bromeliad) and not a moss. Site 13 has more information on Spanish moss.

The "Guns on the River" display at the fort describes the tactical genius of placing a fort on the outside of the bend of a river. This made it impossible for oncoming war vessels to point their sideward-facing cannons at the fort before the boat was well within range of the fort cannons. But, where the fort may have escaped peril at the hands of man, it was placed in jeopardy at the whimsy of the meandering Frederica River. As you may recall from the explanation in the Salt Marsh section on meandering, page 29 and 30, the outer bank of the bend of a marsh river tends to erode. Already a third of the fort has been lost to erosion and thousands of dollars have been spent in attempts to halt further loss.

After exploring the fort, walk to the Barracks, the large tabby ruin across the field, which is next on the path to be visited. After visiting the Barracks, continue walking toward the moat at the edge of the woods. As you approach the moat, three gnarled live oaks entwined with heavy muscadine vines make a picturesque sight. Across the moat and east about 100 feet from the oaks is an immense loblolly pine of great age. Few loblollies grow to this size, because they are either cut for timber or destroyed by pine bark beetles. Follow the moat to the corner, where the Town Bastion and Town Wall displays are located. The walk from the corner of the moat to the interpretive center offers a spectacular view of some of the island's greatest live oaks. Walk slowly in or beside the moat and frequently stop to take in the august shapes of these trees.

Ladies' Tresses

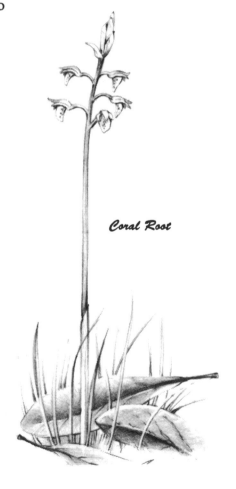

Coral Root

Site #15: Taylor's Fish Camp

Areas: Boat dock on a tidal river, fields and oak groves on Cannon's Point Plantation

The entrance to Taylor's Fish Camp is on Cannon's Point Road, which is the right fork off Lawrence Road, three miles north of the turn-off to Christ Church. The sandy road to the fish camp leads you through young woods and pastureland. The fields do not become visible until you take the right turn to the fish camp.

The smaller sand road going straight leads to the ruins of John Couper's Plantation House, which is not open to the public. The bucolic setting of the grand live oaks, festooned with Spanish moss, and the open fields surrounding the fish camp, makes it difficult to believe that you are still on St. Simons Island.

Actually, this is representative of what most of the island was like during the antebellum years (see Plantation Period of the History section). The fish camp dock is located at the end of the road. The managers of the fish camp conduct fishing and touring excursions in the marsh backwaters. Many regulars come here to put in their boats and fish, but you are encouraged to simply dwell here, enjoy the view, walk about the grounds and have a picnic under the circular grove of moss-laden live oaks.

From the dock, you can see Little St. Simons Island across the marsh. To the southeast, the Hampton River and the north end of Sea Island are visible. Site 15 in Figure 1 should be helpful in locating these areas. Within the grove of live oaks, Seville orange trees, believed to have been brought over by the Spanish in the 16th century, are still bearing fruit. In a field across from the dock are the remains of the one-room schoolhouse, used in the filming of the movie "Conrack" in the early 1970s (see title drawing). A short way back on the sand road from the dock is a renovated tabby slave cabin, which is currently being used as an art studio by Peggy Buchan, the wife of the camp manager. You may see some of the piglets from this year's litters of wild pigs, that have been with the Buchans over the years. The black, tan and brindle colors, small stature and long snouts are characteristic of the wild pigs of the coastal Southeast.

Site #16: Sea Island Road

Area: The western shore of St. Simons Island, seen from Sea Island Road

The features of this site are best viewed traveling west on Sea Island Road, from the Frederica Road intersection to Demere Road. About a 1/4 mile out on Sea Island Road from the intersection, you cross the bridge over Dunbar Creek.

Just after crossing the bridge, park on the right shoulder. Looking back to the east, you see the western shoreline of St. Simons Island. From your position and from the map, Figure 19, you see that loops of Dunbar Creek meander close to the western shore. Over the years, the erosion from this meandering creek has cut away hundreds of acres of upland, giving this shoreline its irregular shape. Look at Figure 19 to appreciate the immense amount of upland that was eroded away between Ft. Frederica, Epworth Acres, and Redfern Village. From the bridge, the headland, where Fort Frederica is located, is seen extending out from the shoreline, about a mile to the north, beyond the shorter headland with houses.

A northern branch of Dunbar Creek formed the wetlands that penetrate the central and northern parts of St. Simons Island (see Figure 1). The ponds and swamps near Christ Church, described in Site 13, are part of this wetland system.

South of the bridge, Dunbar Creek marsh cleaves deeply into the southern end of St. Simons Island. The extreme southern end of this marsh is visible from Redfern Village and from Demere Road, just west of its intersection with Frederica Road. Many of the ponds and low areas in the neighborhoods west of Frederica Road are part of Dunbar's wetlands.

Proceeding along Sea Island Road, you become aware of many tree-covered hammocks. These are the fragments of upland, left behind from the meandering activities of Dunbar Creek. As you approach the bend, the road cuts through one of the hammocks, giving you a close-up view of the type of plant communities on these marsh islands.

Most of the marsh on the southern and eastern sides of the road is covered with the coarse, black-colored needle rush. In the Salt Marsh section, needle rush is described as an indicator plant for lower salt concentration in a marsh. The combination of the roadbed obstructing tidal circulation and the freshwater runoff from the surrounding uplands, contributes to the reduced salt concentration of this side of the marsh. The land seen in the distance across the marsh to the west is the mainland, north of Brunswick.

PLANT IDENTIFICATION

The plants are grouped as they appear in the various zones of each of the barrier island's ecosystems. Brief descriptions of identifying features for each plant and its flowering season are presented at the bottom of each page of illustrations. Where a plant equally inhabits other ecosystems besides the one in which it is illustrated, the other ecosystems are given in parentheses at the end of the identifying descriptions. In order to conserve space, the plant illustrations are not drawn to scale.

Ocean Beach

Upper Beach
(Pioneer plants)

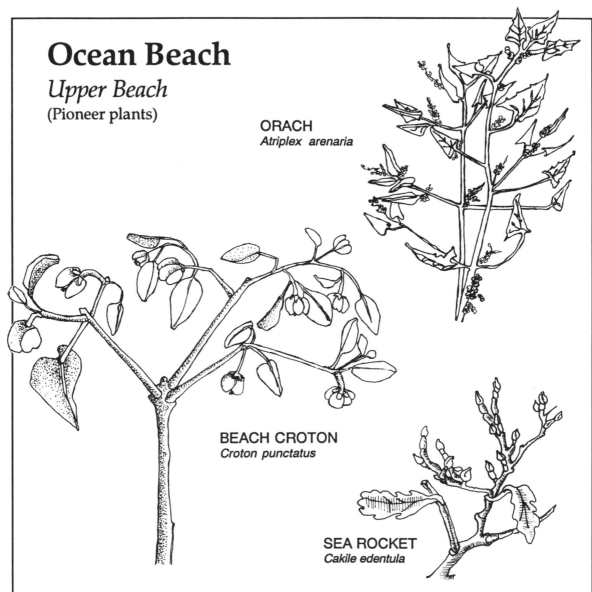

ORACH
Atriplex arenaria

BEACH CROTON
Croton punctatus

SEA ROCKET
Cakile edentula

ORACH: succulent gray-green leaf, red stem, summer.
BEACH CROTON: dusky gray-green leaves and stem, round fruit, spring.
SEA ROCKET: succulent plant, two-section fruit, dies in summer, spring.

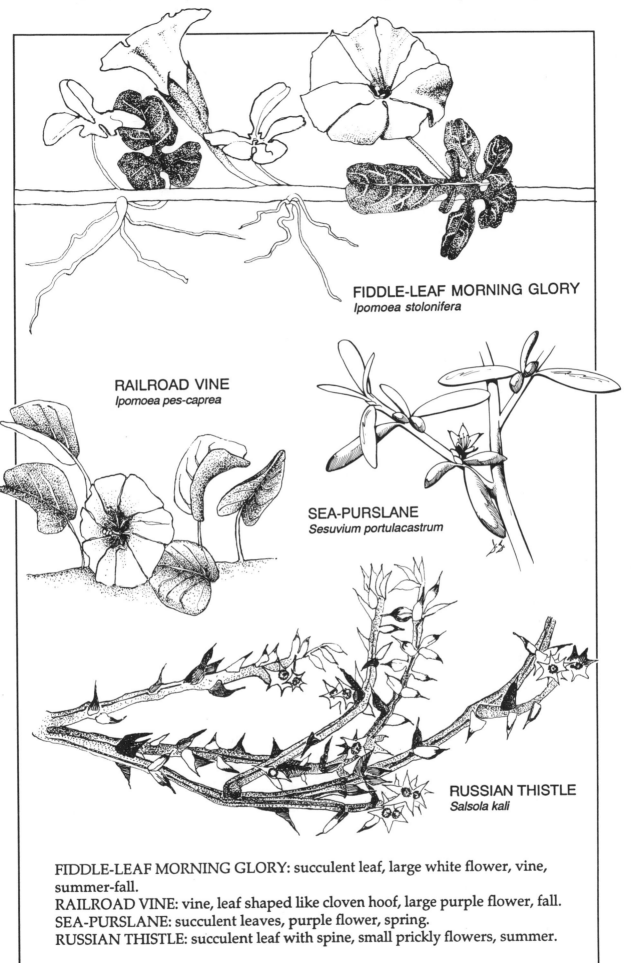

FIDDLE-LEAF MORNING GLORY
Ipomoea stolonifera

RAILROAD VINE
Ipomoea pes-caprea

SEA-PURSLANE
Sesuvium portulacastrum

RUSSIAN THISTLE
Salsola kali

FIDDLE-LEAF MORNING GLORY: succulent leaf, large white flower, vine, summer-fall.
RAILROAD VINE: vine, leaf shaped like cloven hoof, large purple flower, fall.
SEA-PURSLANE: succulent leaves, purple flower, spring.
RUSSIAN THISTLE: succulent leaf with spine, small prickly flowers, summer.

Primary Dunes

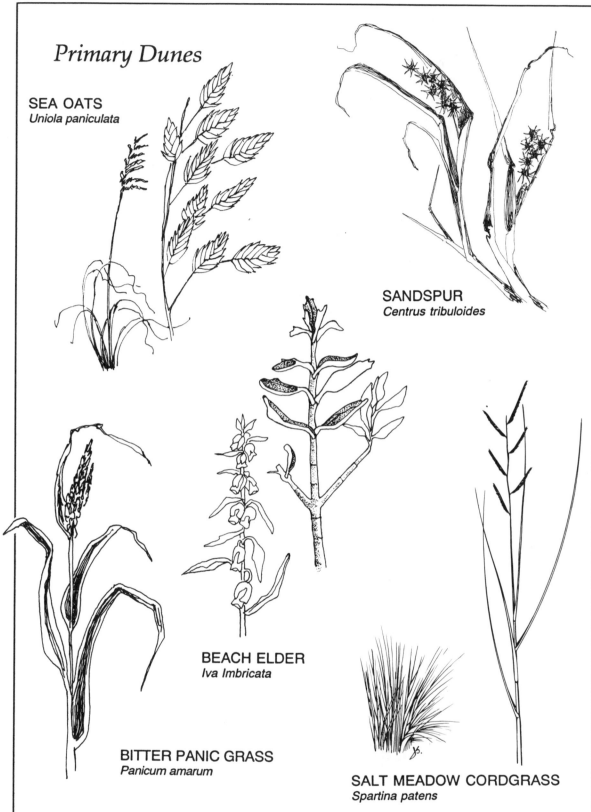

SEA OATS
Uniola paniculata

SANDSPUR
Centrus tribuloides

BEACH ELDER
Iva Imbricata

BITTER PANIC GRASS
Panicum amarum

SALT MEADOW CORDGRASS
Spartina patens

SEA OATS: seed head on tall stalk, curly leaf blade, summer-fall.
SANDSPUR: prostrate, sharp painful burr, fall.
BEACH ELDER: succulent leaf, woody stem, summer.
BITTER PANIC GRASS: broad, alternate leaf blades on the stalk, summer.
SALT MEADOW CORDGRASS: narrow leaf blade, summer (saltmarsh).
DROPSEED GRASS: (not shown) similar to salt grass (see Salt Marsh).

Dune Meadows

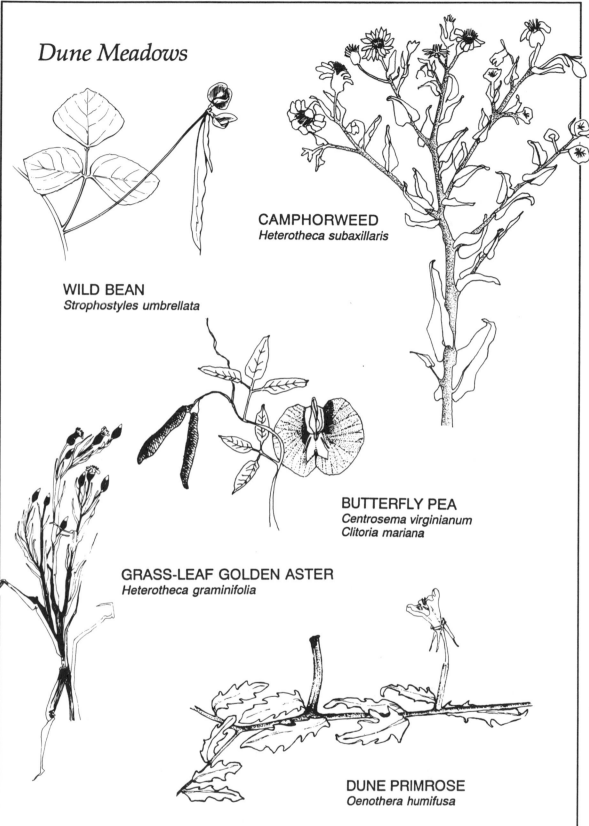

CAMPHORWEED
Heterotheca subaxillaris

WILD BEAN
Strophostyles umbrellata

BUTTERFLY PEA
Centrosema virginianum
Clitoria mariana

GRASS-LEAF GOLDEN ASTER
Heterotheca graminifolia

DUNE PRIMROSE
Oenothera humifusa

CAMPHORWEED: yellow aster flower, fall.
WILD BEAN: small red pea flower, slender black pod, vine, summer-fall.
BUTTERFLY PEA: large purple pea flower, vine, spring-fall (edge of woods).
GRASS-LEAF GOLDEN ASTER: yellow aster flower, grass-like leaf, summer.
DUNE PRIMROSE: prostrate, pink and yellow flower, spring-fall (fields).

Dune Meadows

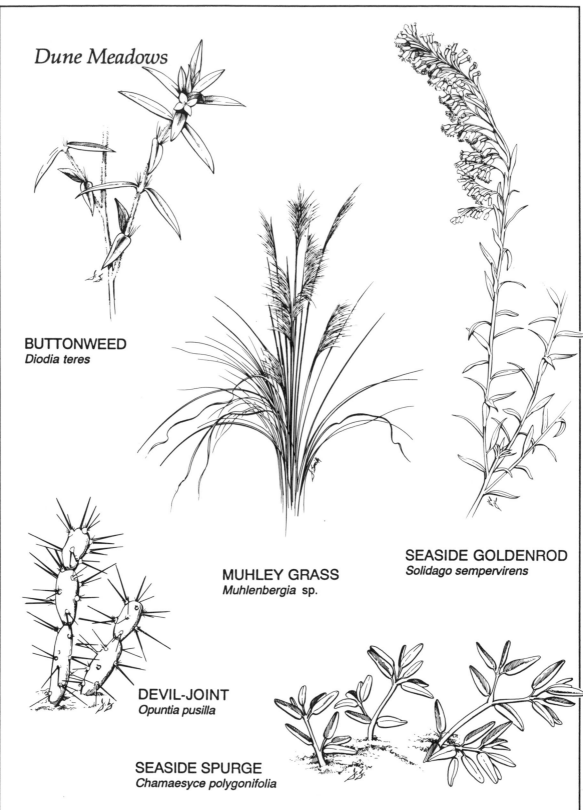

BUTTONWEED
Diodia teres

MUHLEY GRASS
Muhlenbergia sp.

SEASIDE GOLDENROD
Solidago sempervirens

DEVIL-JOINT
Opuntia pusilla

SEASIDE SPURGE
Chamaesyce polygonifolia

BUTTONWEED: prostrate, white four-petaled flower, summer-fall (fields).
SEASIDE GOLDENROD: tall, many golden flowers, fall (fields).
MUHLEY GRASS: many, tiny, lavender flowers on long, wispy panicles, fall
(fields and sloughs).
DEVIL-JOINT: small prickly-pear cactus, barbed spines, spring (fields).
SEASIDE SPURGE: small plant, opposite leaves, prostrate, summer.

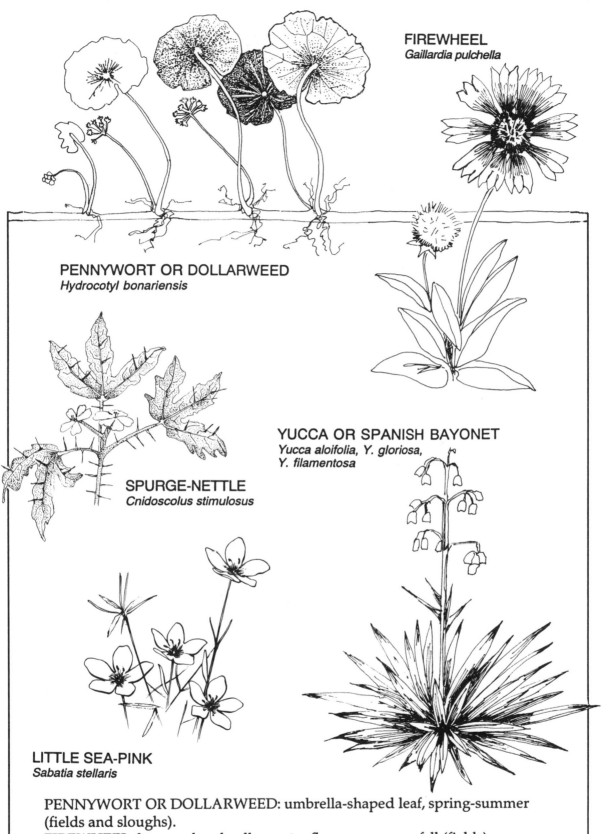

FIREWHEEL
Gaillardia pulchella

PENNYWORT OR DOLLARWEED
Hydrocotyl bonariensis

YUCCA OR SPANISH BAYONET
Yucca aloifolia, Y. gloriosa,
Y. filamentosa

SPURGE-NETTLE
Cnidoscolus stimulosus

LITTLE SEA-PINK
Sabatia stellaris

PENNYWORT OR DOLLARWEED: umbrella-shaped leaf, spring-summer
(fields and sloughs).
FIREWHEEL: large red and yellow aster flower, summer-fall (fields).
SPURGE-NETTLE: small white flower, nettles, spring-summer (fields).
LITTLE SEA-PINK: small pink flower with yellow center, summer.
YUCCA OR SPANISH BAYONET: succulent leaf with sharp point, summer
(fields).

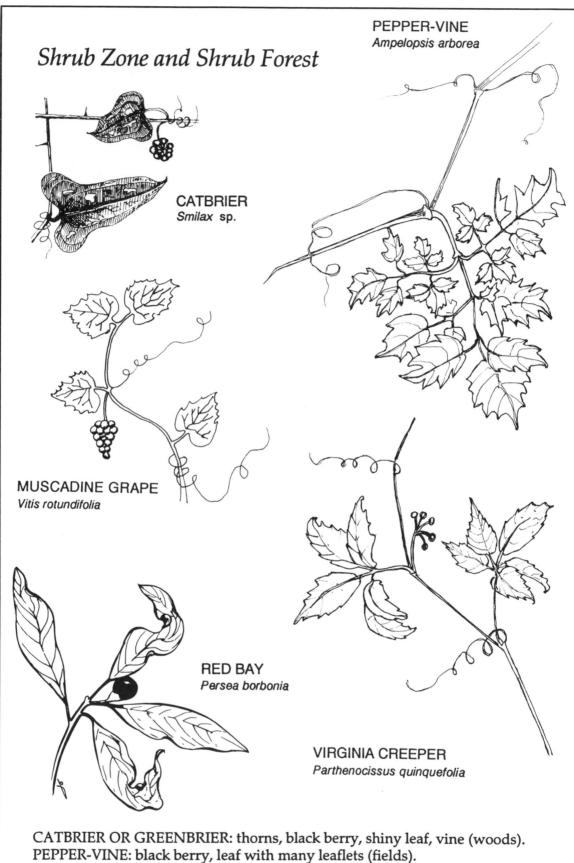

Shrub Zone and Shrub Forest

PEPPER-VINE
Ampelopsis arborea

CATBRIER
Smilax sp.

MUSCADINE GRAPE
Vitis rotundifolia

RED BAY
Persea borbonia

VIRGINIA CREEPER
Parthenocissus quinquefolia

CATBRIER OR GREENBRIER: thorns, black berry, shiny leaf, vine (woods).
PEPPER-VINE: black berry, leaf with many leaflets (fields).
MUSCADINE GRAPE: grapes, vine (woods).
RED BAY: aromatic leaf, tree (woods).
VIRGINIA CREEPER: leaf has five leaflets, vine (woods).

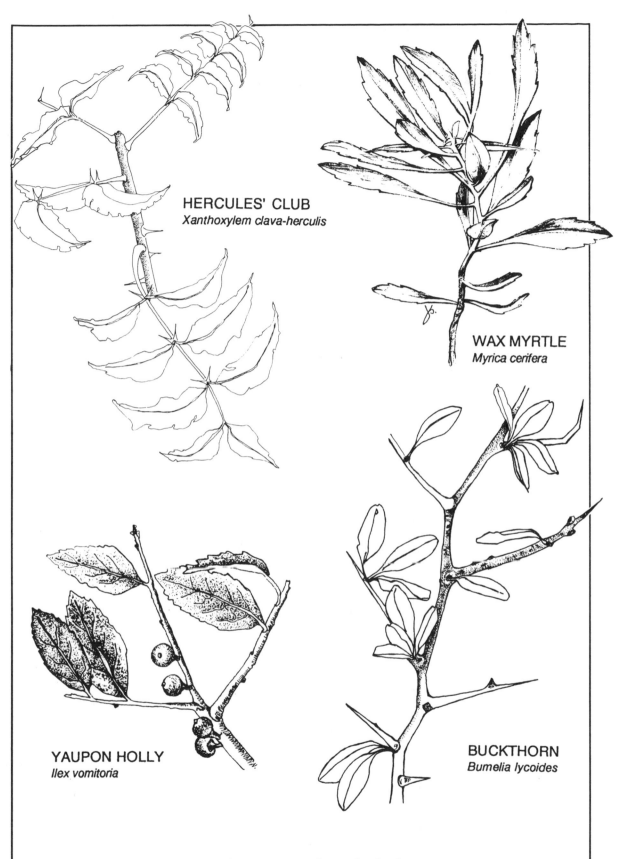

HERCULES' CLUB
Xanthoxylem clava-herculis

WAX MYRTLE
Myrica cerifera

YAUPON HOLLY
Ilex vomitoria

BUCKTHORN
Bumelia lycoides

HERCULES' CLUB: pointed warty growths on bark, thorns.
WAX MYRTLE: shrub, aromatic, clusters of small gray berries (woods).
YAUPON HOLLY: shrub, shiny evergreen leaf, red berry in winter, (woods).
BUCKTHORN: thorn often among whorls of leaves, small tree.

Salt Marsh
Low Marsh

SMOOTH CORDGRASS
Spartina   alterniflora

SMOOTH CORDGRASS: broad leaf blade, plant size varies with salinity, fall.

High Marsh

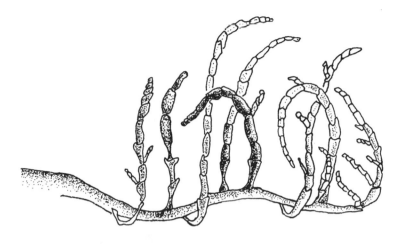

GLASSWORT
Salicornia virginica, S. bigelovii, S. europaea

SALT GRASS
Distichlis spicata

SALTWORT
Batis maritima

GLASSWORT OR PICKLE WEED: succulent plants with tiny
bract-like leaves.
SALT GRASS: leaf blades in one plane, summer-fall (beach meadows).
SALTWORT: succulent leaf, prostrate woody stem.

Marsh Border

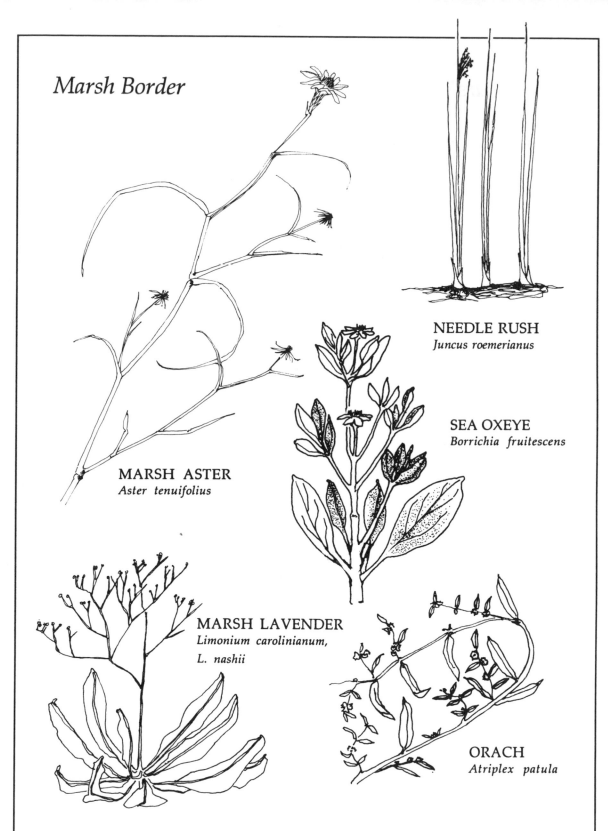

NEEDLE RUSH
Juncus roemerianus

SEA OXEYE
Borrichia fruitescens

MARSH ASTER
Aster tenuifolius

MARSH LAVENDER
Limonium carolinianum,
L. nashii

ORACH
Atriplex patula

MARSH ASTER: small sparsely-arranged lavender or white aster flowers
with yellow centers, fall.
NEEDLE RUSH: long tubular leaves with sharp points, painful to walkers.
SEA OXEYE: succulent leaf, yellow aster flower, spiny burr, summer.
MARSH LAVENDER: small sparsely-arranged purple flowers, basal leaves, fall.
ORACH: similar to orach on beaches (A. arenaria) but smaller leaves.

Upper Marsh Border and Transition Zone

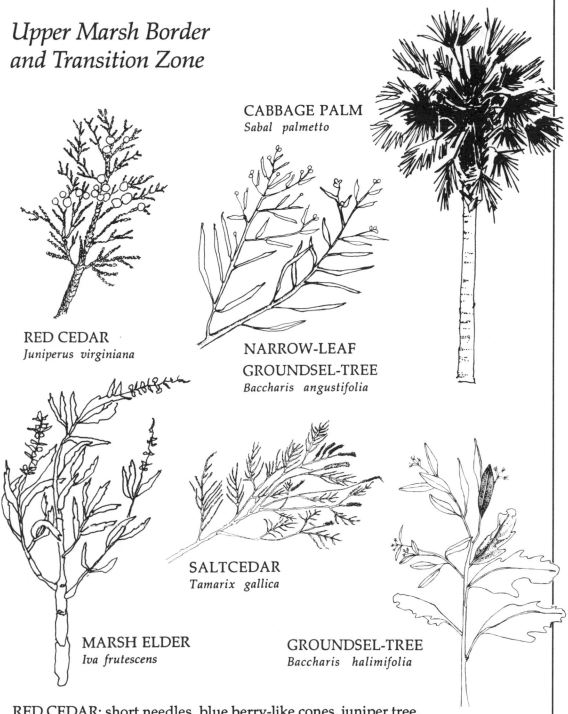

CABBAGE PALM
Sabal palmetto

RED CEDAR
Juniperus virginiana

NARROW-LEAF GROUNDSEL-TREE
Baccharis angustifolia

SALTCEDAR
Tamarix gallica

MARSH ELDER
Iva frutescens

GROUNDSEL-TREE
Baccharis halimifolia

RED CEDAR: short needles, blue berry-like cones, juniper tree.
CABBAGE PALM: similar to saw palmetto of the forest but pinnately-arranged leaves and no spines on leaf stalks, tree.
NARROW-LEAF GROUNDSEL-TREE OR FALSE WILLOW: similar to groundsel-tree but rarer and with narrower leaves.
MARSH ELDER OR HIGH TIDE BUSH: serrated leaves, tiny flowers or seeds at end of stems, leaves not as fleshy as beach elder.
SALTCEDAR OR TAMARISK: small tree or shrub, similar to red cedar but paler green and more delicate, tiny pink flowers at tips of stems, summer.
GROUNDSEL-TREE OR COTTON BUSH: irregularly-shaped leaves, cotton-like seed tufts in the fall, shrub.

Freshwater Slough
Floating and Emergent Plants

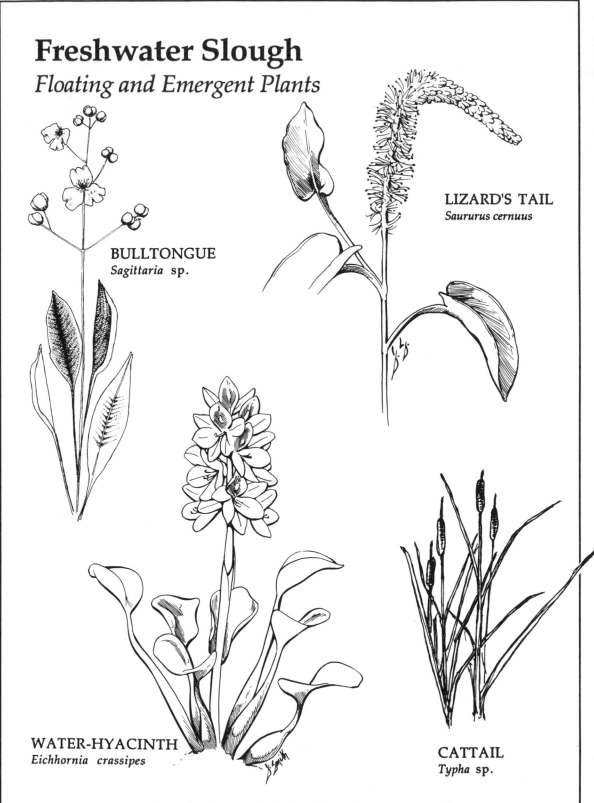

BULLTONGUE
Sagittaria sp.

LIZARD'S TAIL
Saururus cernuus

WATER-HYACINTH
Eichhornia crassipes

CATTAIL
Typha sp.

LIZARD'S TAIL: densely clustered, little white flowers on a spike, summer.
BULLTONGUE: sparsely-arranged white flowers on a spike, summer-fall.
CATTAIL: tall plants, narrow leaves, large brown hot dog-shaped flower heads, summer-fall.
WATER-HYACINTH: ornate blue flowers, inflated leaf bases, summer.

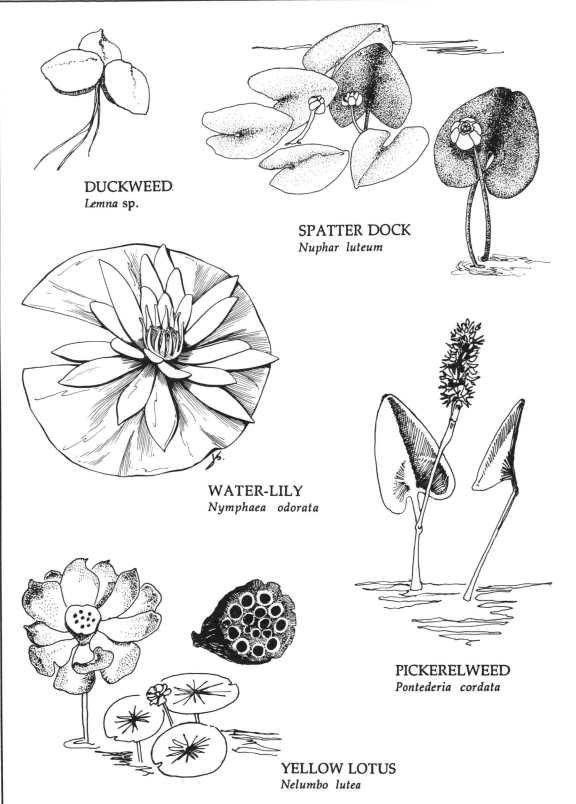

DUCKWEED.
Lemna sp.

SPATTER DOCK
Nuphar luteum

WATER-LILY
Nymphaea odorata

PICKERELWEED
Pontederia cordata

YELLOW LOTUS
Nelumbo lutea

DUCKWEED: tiny floating plants, often covering surfaces of ponds.
SPATTER DOCK: yellow spherical flower, spring-fall.
WATER-LILY: large white or pink fragrant flower with yellow center,
spring-summer.
PICKERELWEED: cylindrical blue flower head, summer-fall.
YELLOW LOTUS: yellow flower, large shower head-shaped seed pod,
umbrella-shaped leaves, summer.

Wetland Plants

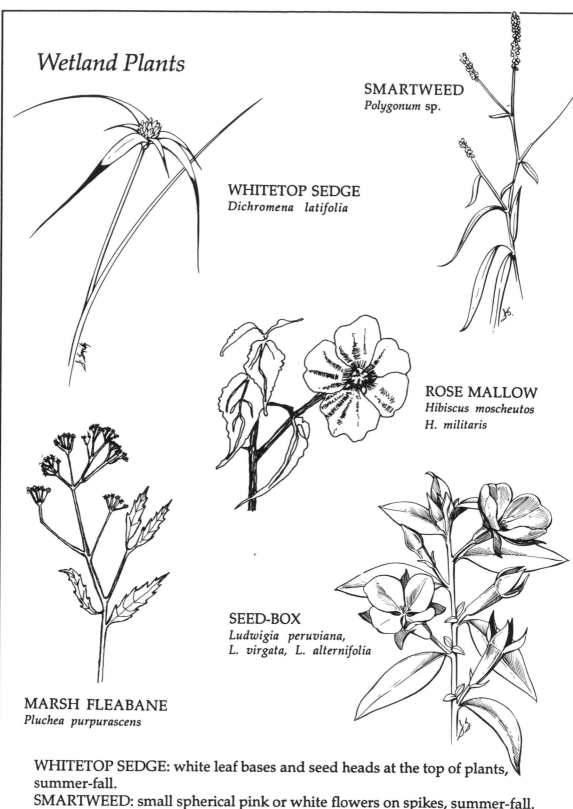

SMARTWEED
Polygonum sp.

WHITETOP SEDGE
Dichromena latifolia

ROSE MALLOW
Hibiscus moscheutos
H. militaris

SEED-BOX
Ludwigia peruviana,
L. virgata, L. alternifolia

MARSH FLEABANE
Pluchea purpurascens

WHITETOP SEDGE: white leaf bases and seed heads at the top of plants, summer-fall.

SMARTWEED: small spherical pink or white flowers on spikes, summer-fall.

ROSE MALLOW OR MARSH MALLOW: tall plant, large pink or white hibiscus flowers, summer-fall.

SEED-BOX: four-petaled yellow flowers, sizes of plants and flowers vary greatly with species, summer-fall.

MARSH FLEABANE OR CAMPHORWEED: heads of lavender aster flowers, summer-fall.

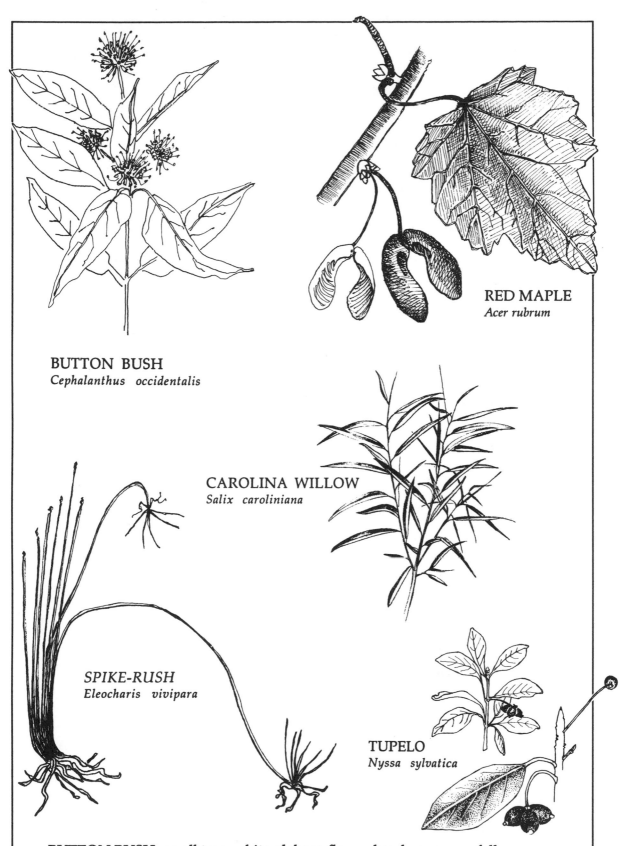

RED MAPLE
Acer rubrum

BUTTON BUSH
Cephalanthus occidentalis

CAROLINA WILLOW
Salix caroliniana

SPIKE-RUSH
Eleocharis vivipara

TUPELO
Nyssa sylvatica

BUTTON BUSH: small tree, white globose flower heads, summer-fall.
RED MAPLE: red leaf stalks, red winged fruits (forest).
CAROLINA WILLOW: a short-leaved willow on water-saturated soils.
SPIKE-RUSH: many species of delicate rushes with terminal seed heads.
This particular species has reclining stems with new shoots at stem tips.
TUPELO OR BLACKGUM: small elliptical leaf, small black berry.

Forest
Canopy

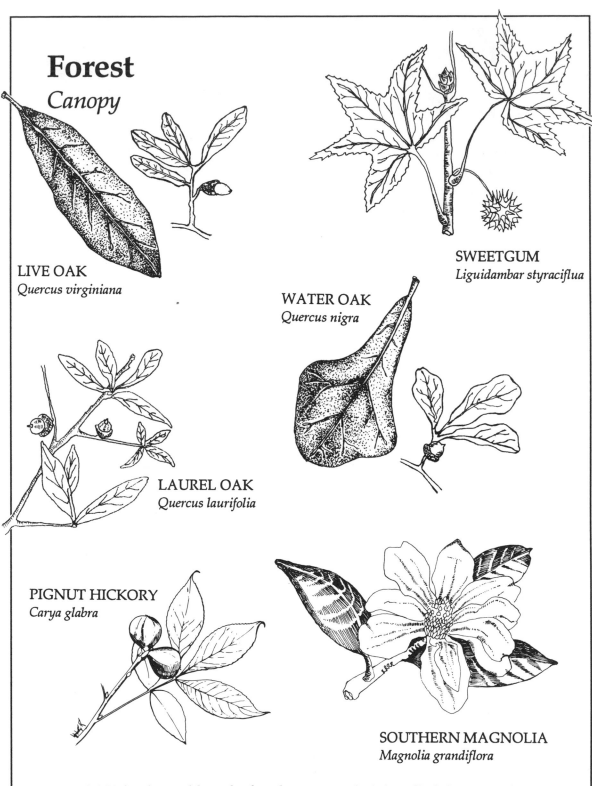

LIVE OAK
Quercus virginiana

SWEETGUM
Liquidambar styraciflua

WATER OAK
Quercus nigra

LAUREL OAK
Quercus laurifolia

PIGNUT HICKORY
Carya glabra

SOUTHERN MAGNOLIA
Magnolia grandiflora

LIVE OAK: leathery oblong leaf with margins slightly rolled downward, black narrow acorn.
SWEETGUM: five-pointed leaves, round spiny gum balls (wetlands).
WATER OAK: spatula-shaped leaf, stout yellow-brown acorn.
LAUREL OAK: narrow elliptical leaf, brown stout acorn.
PIGNUT HICKORY: leaf usually contains five leaflets, hard pear-shaped nut.
SOUTHERN MAGNOLIA: large shiny leaf with rust-colored underside, fruit with red seeds, huge white flowers, spring.

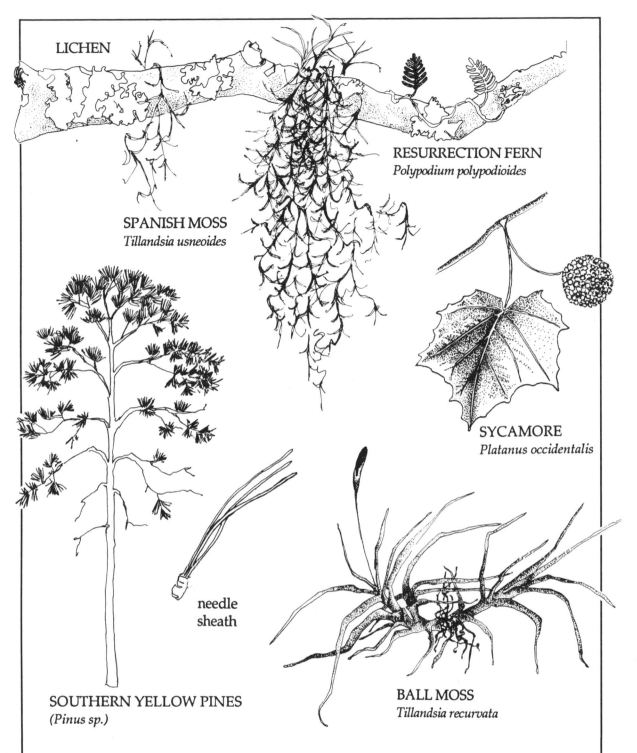

LICHEN

RESURRECTION FERN
Polypodium polypodioides

SPANISH MOSS
Tillandsia usneoides

SYCAMORE
Platanus occidentalis

needle
sheath

SOUTHERN YELLOW PINES
(Pinus sp.)

BALL MOSS
Tillandsia recurvata

EPIPHYTES: SPANISH MOSS, BALL MOSS, RESURRECTION FERN, LICHEN.
SYCAMORE: blotched bark, maple-like leaf, round many-faceted balls.
SOUTHERN YELLOW PINES (Pinus sp.):
    SLASH PINE (P. elliotti): mostly two needles per sheath, cones on short stalks, gray bark.
    LOBLOLLY (P. taeda): mostly three needles per sheath, cones with no stalks, reddish bark.
    LONG-LEAF (P. palustris): mostly three needles per sheath, needles and cones larger than the other pines.
    POND PINES (P. serotina): three to four needles per sheath, small cone.

Understory

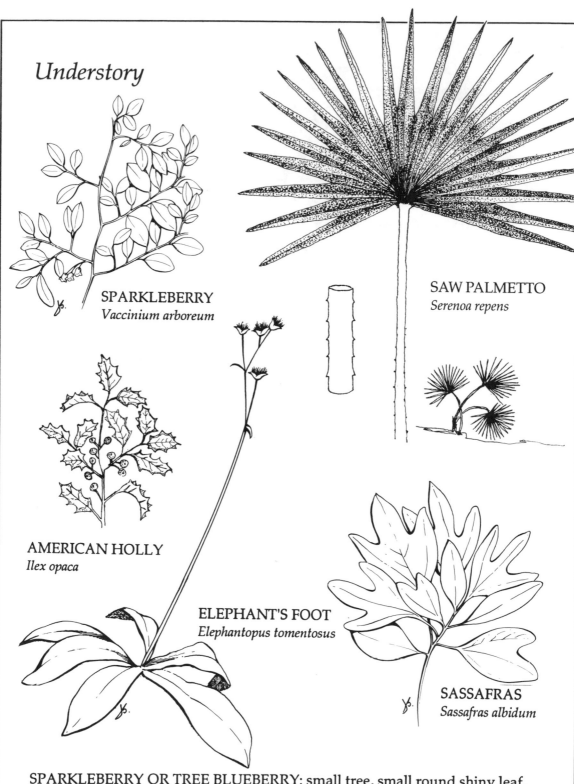

SPARKLEBERRY
Vaccinium arboreum

SAW PALMETTO
Serenoa repens

AMERICAN HOLLY
Ilex opaca

ELEPHANT'S FOOT
Elephantopus tomentosus

SASSAFRAS
Sassafras albidum

SPARKLEBERRY OR TREE BLUEBERRY: small tree, small round shiny leaf, clusters of pink and white bell-shaped flowers, black berry, spring.
SAW PALMETTO: stems grow along the surface of ground, saw-toothed margins on leaf stalks, leaflets grow out from center (palmate), shrub.
AMERICAN HOLLY: small to middle-sized tree, spiny leaf, red berries.
ELEPHANT'S FOOT: rosette of hairy basal leaves, small cluster of modest purple flowers at the end of a long stalk, summer-fall.
SASSAFRAS: small tree, irregularly-lobed leaf (often mitten-shaped), distinct odor.

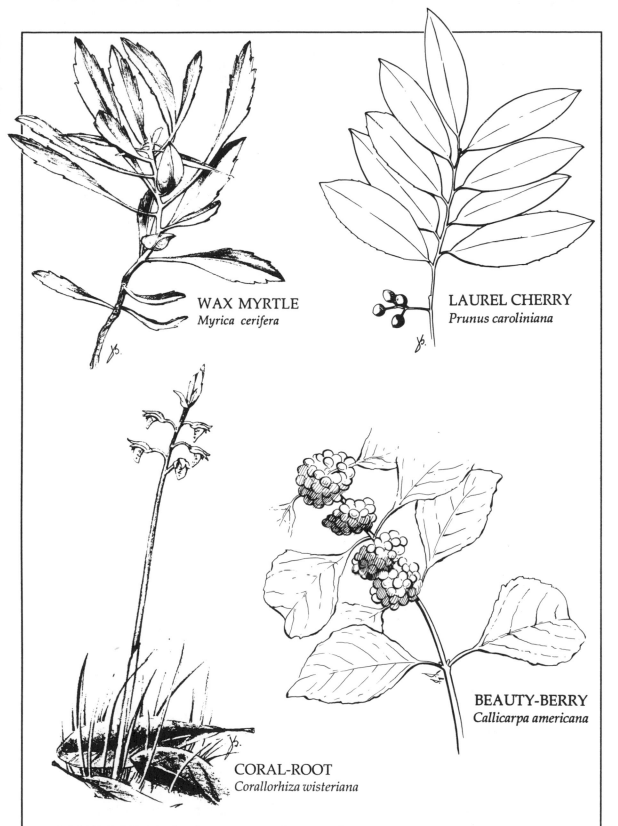

WAX MYRTLE
Myrica cerifera

LAUREL CHERRY
Prunus caroliniana

CORAL-ROOT
Corallorhiza wisteriana

BEAUTY-BERRY
Callicarpa americana

WAX MYRTLE: shrub, aromatic, clusters of small gray berries (beach).
LAUREL CHERRY: small to middle-sized **tree**, shiny leaf often with sharp
small points on leaf margin, black berry.
CORAL-ROOT: rust-colored orchid consisting of a stalk bearing a few small
flowers, no leaves, found in leaf-litter under oaks, spring.
BEAUTY-BERRY: shrub, spherical clusters of purple-magenta flowers and
berries at the leaf axes, spring.

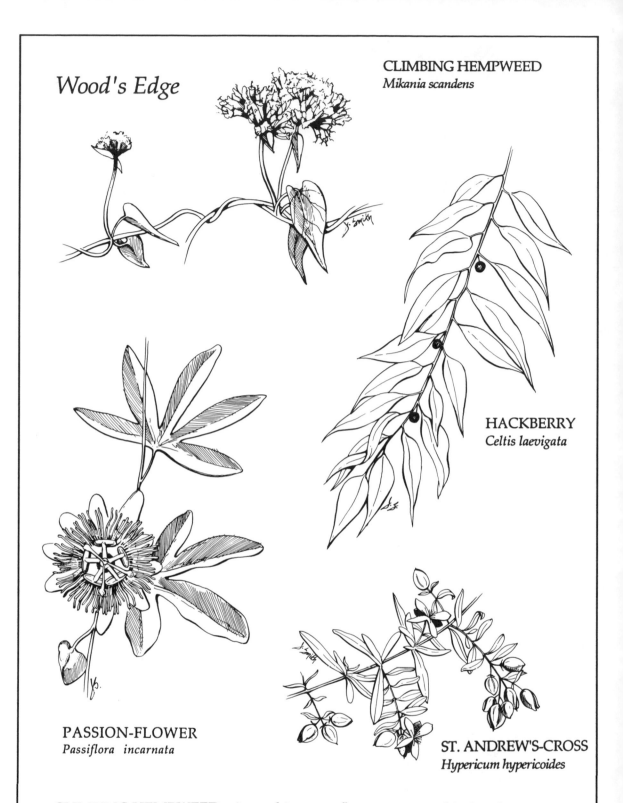

Wood's Edge

CLIMBING HEMPWEED
Mikania scandens

HACKBERRY
Celtis laevigata

PASSION-FLOWER
Passiflora incarnata

ST. ANDREW'S-CROSS
Hypericum hypericoides

CLIMBING HEMPWEED: vine, white aster flowers arranged in heads, summer-fall (fields).
HACKBERRY: shrub or tree, leaves alternate and arranged in one plane, small red-brown fruit, bark ash-gray often with spiny growths (fields).
PASSION-FLOWER OR MAYPOP: vine, distinctive complex blue flowers, green passion fruit, summer-fall.
ST. ANDREW'S-CROSS: narrow four-petaled flower, disk-shaped pod, summer-fall (fields).

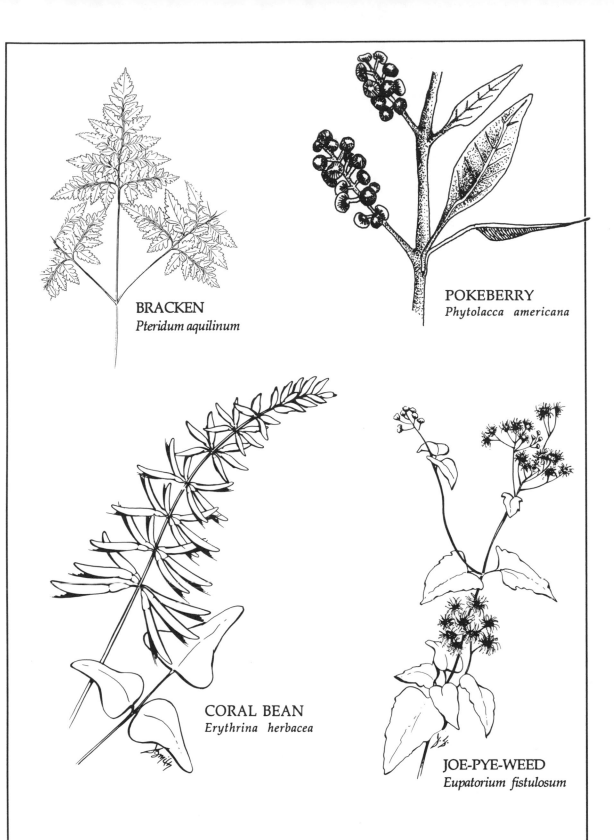

BRACKEN
Pteridum aquilinum

POKEBERRY
Phytolacca americana

CORAL BEAN
Erythrina herbacea

JOE-PYE-WEED
Eupatorium fistulosum

BRACKEN: medium-sized brittle fern, three-branched leaves (fields).
POKEBERRY: large leafy weed, clusters of black berries (fields).
CORAL BEAN: leaves having three pear-shaped leaflets, spikes of elongated red flowers, spring-summer (fields).
JOE-PYE-WEED: stems and leaves wooly, purple flower heads, fall (sloughs, fields).

Fields and Roadsides

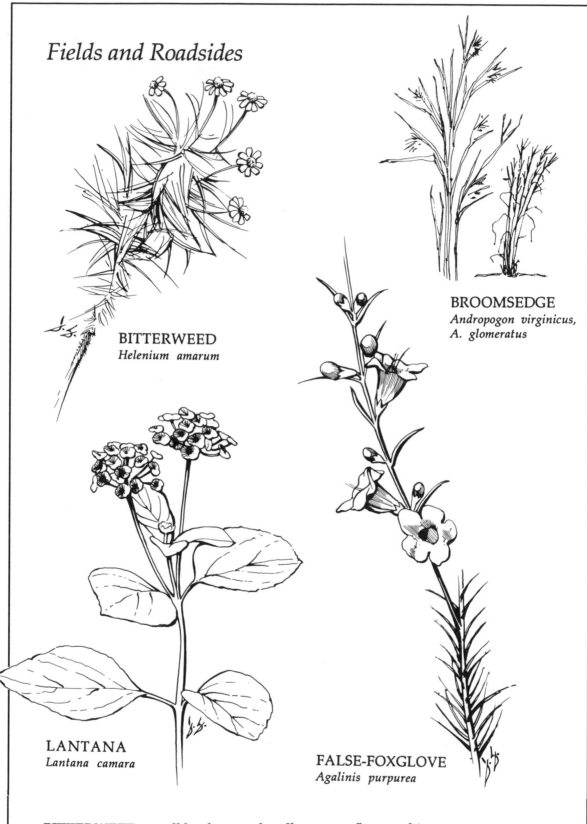

BITTERWEED
Helenium amarum

BROOMSEDGE
*Andropogon virginicus,
A. glomeratus*

LANTANA
Lantana camara

FALSE-FOXGLOVE
Agalinis purpurea

BITTERWEED: small bushy weed, yellow aster flowers, bitter taste, summer.
BROOMSEDGE: rust-colored grass, white seed tufts in fall.
LANTANA: shrub, yellow and orange (or pink) flowers on heads, summer-fall.
FALSE-FOXGLOVE OR GERARDIA: purple to pink trumpet-shaped flowers.
Flowers grow at leaf axes throughout the length of the branch, fall.

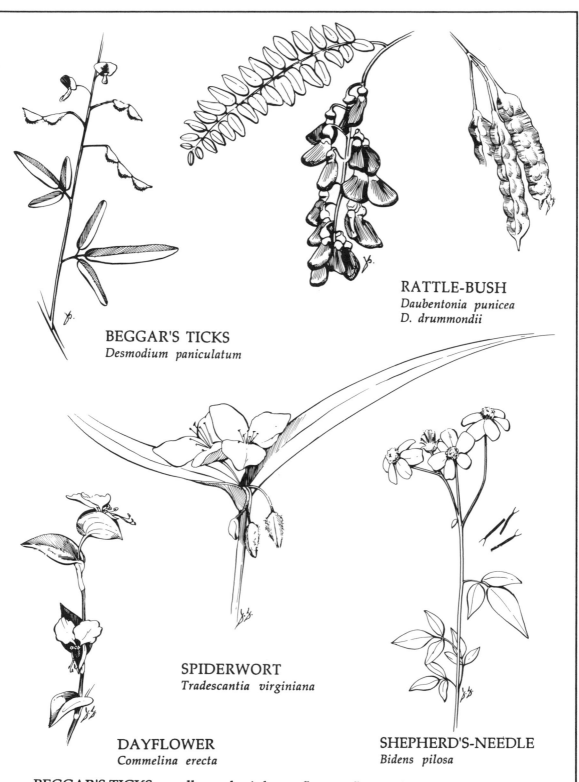

RATTLE-BUSH
Daubentonia punicea
D. drummondii

BEGGAR'S TICKS
Desmodium paniculatum

SPIDERWORT
Tradescantia virginiana

DAYFLOWER
Commelina erecta

SHEPHERD'S-NEEDLE
Bidens pilosa

BEGGAR'S TICKS: small weed, pink pea flower, flat seed pods whose triangular segments easily break off and stick to clothing, summer-fall.
RATTLE-BUSH: *D. punicea* has orange-red pea flowers, *D. drummondii* has yellow flowers, both have winged pods, summer-fall.
SPIDERWORT: clusters of blue three-petaled flowers, spring-summer.
DAYFLOWER: flowers with two blue petals and third greatly reduced, summer.
SHEPHERD'S-NEEDLE: white aster flower with yellow center, barbed needle-like seeds which stick to clothing, all year.

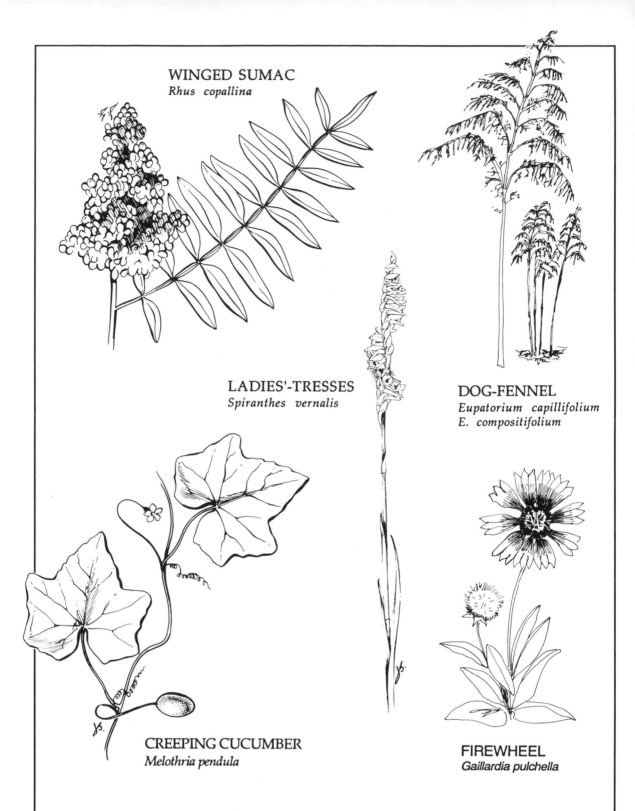

WINGED SUMAC
Rhus copallina

LADIES'-TRESSES
Spiranthes vernalis

DOG-FENNEL
Eupatorium capillifolium
E. compositifolium

CREEPING CUCUMBER
Melothria pendula

FIREWHEEL
Gaillardia pulchella

WINGED SUMAC: shrub, narrow wings on leaf stems, clusters of dull-red flowers, fall.
DOG-FENNEL: tall weed, many small white flowers on pointed heads at the top of branches, fall.
CREEPING CUCUMBER: vine, small three-lobed leaf, small yellow flower, miniature cucumber (poisonous), summer-fall.
LADIES' TRESSES: orchid, small spirally-arranged white flowers, spring.
FIREWHEEL: large red and yellow aster flower, summer-fall (beach meadow).

ANIMAL IDENTIFICATION

The animals identified in this section are limited to commonly-seen inverte-brates living on ocean beaches and salt marshes and in their nearshore waters. There are excellent field guides which cover other animal phyla, and identify seashells and other animal remains washed up onto the beach. Brief descriptons of the invertebrate, its burrow or other evidence of its presence are given at the bottom of each page. Where an invertebrate is commonly found in an ecosystem other than the one designated, the other appears in parentheses at the end of the description. The animal illustrations are not drawn to scale.

Ocean Beach

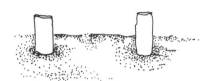

ONUPHIS WORM burrows
Onuphis sp.

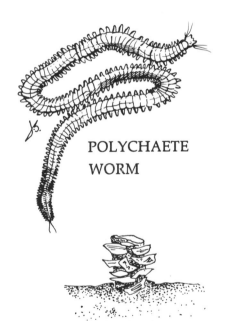

POLYCHAETE
WORM

PLUMED WORM burrow
Diapatra cuprea

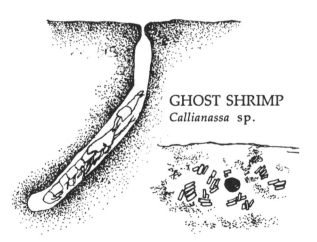

GHOST SHRIMP
Callianassa sp.

GHOST SHRIMP burrow
with fecal pellets

POLYCHAETE WORM: many species varying in size and appearance on shore and in aquatic environments.
ONUPHIS WORM: parchment-like burrow entrance, in low tide zone, the polychaete rarely seen.
PLUMED WORM: burrow entrance with shell and plant fragments attached, in low tide zone, the polychaete rarely seen.
GHOST SHRIMP: burrow often surrounded by small fecal pellets, in low tide zone, animal 3-to 5-inch-long white-pinkish body, the animal rarely seen (marsh).

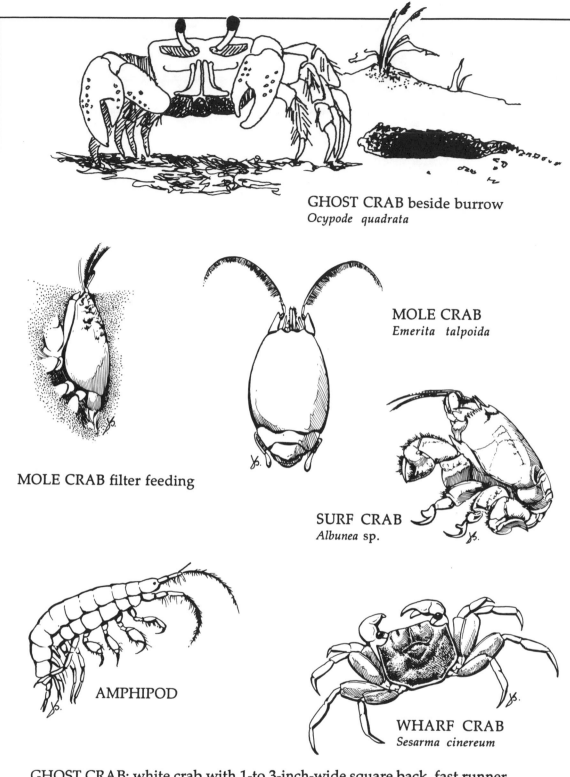

GHOST CRAB beside burrow
Ocypode quadrata

MOLE CRAB
Emerita talpoida

MOLE CRAB filter feeding

SURF CRAB
Albunea sp.

AMPHIPOD

WHARF CRAB
Sesarma cinereum

GHOST CRAB: white crab with 1-to 3-inch-wide square back, fast runner, more commonly seen at night, burrow in upper beach.
MOLE CRAB: 1-inch-long egg-shaped white crab, seen just below surface of sand in the swash zone, in the northern and southern regions.
SURF CRAB OR MOLE CRAB: stouter and shaped differently than the other mole crab and found in same habitat, southern species.
AMPHIPOD: many species in shore and aquatic environments.
WHARF CRAB: 1/2-inch brown square-backed crab, often found among tidal wrack (marsh).

LETTERED OLIVE
Oliva sayana

MOON SNAIL
Polinices duplicatus

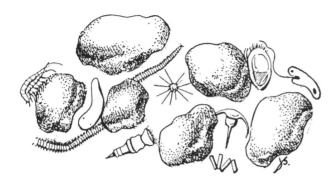

PSAMMON

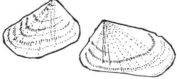

COQUINA CLAM
Donax sp.

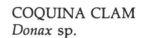

SAND DOLLAR
Mellita quinquiesperforata

LETTERED OLIVE: elongated glassy-smooth shell with V-shaped markings, crawls just under the surface of sand leaving convoluted trails visible in the low tide zone, feeds on coquina clams.
MOON SNAIL: almost spherical shell with large opening, leaves trails similar to the lettered olive in low tide zone, leaves small beveled holes in bivalve and other moon snail shells after feeding.
PSAMMON: tiny plants and animals which live among the sand grains.
COQUINA CLAM: small, roughly triangular shell of varying colors, found in the surf zone.
SAND DOLLAR: brown flat urchin with short bristle-like spines, five openings in shell, seen just below surface of sand in shallow water.

Salt Marsh
Molluscs

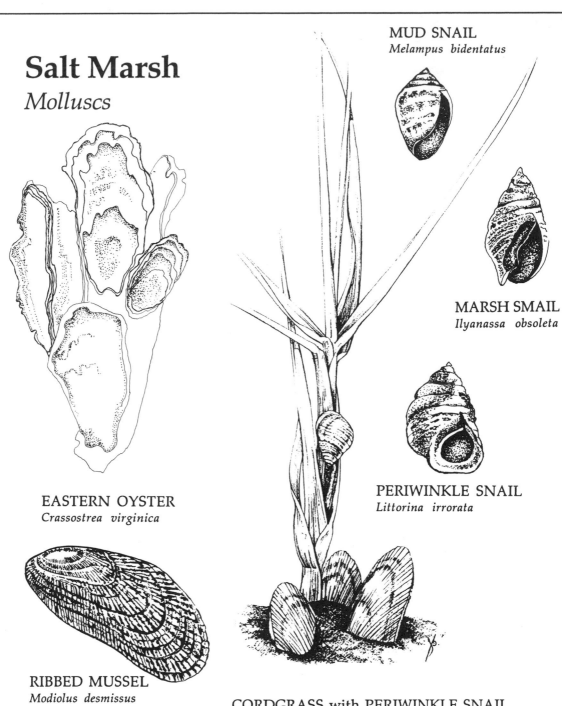

MUD SNAIL
Melampus bidentatus

MARSH SMAIL
Ilyanassa obsoleta

PERIWINKLE SNAIL
Littorina irrorata

EASTERN OYSTER
Crassostrea virginica

RIBBED MUSSEL
Modiolus desmissus

CORDGRASS with PERIWINKLE SNAIL
on stem, RIBBED MUSSELS at base.

OYSTERS: gray irregularly-shaped shell, often found in clusters attached to root masses or other firm surfaces (rocks on beach).

RIBBED MUSSEL: gray to brown shell, attached to cordgrass or other firm surfaces by bysasus threads, usually partially buried in mud (rocks on beach).

MUD SNAIL OR COFFEE-BEAN SNAIL: 1/2-inch-long black shell, often found close to plants or detritus near the high tide line.

MARSH SNAIL:1-inch-long black shell, shell often partially corroded, thousands often seen on tidal flats.

PERIWINKLE SNAIL: white snail found on cordgrass stalks.

Crabs

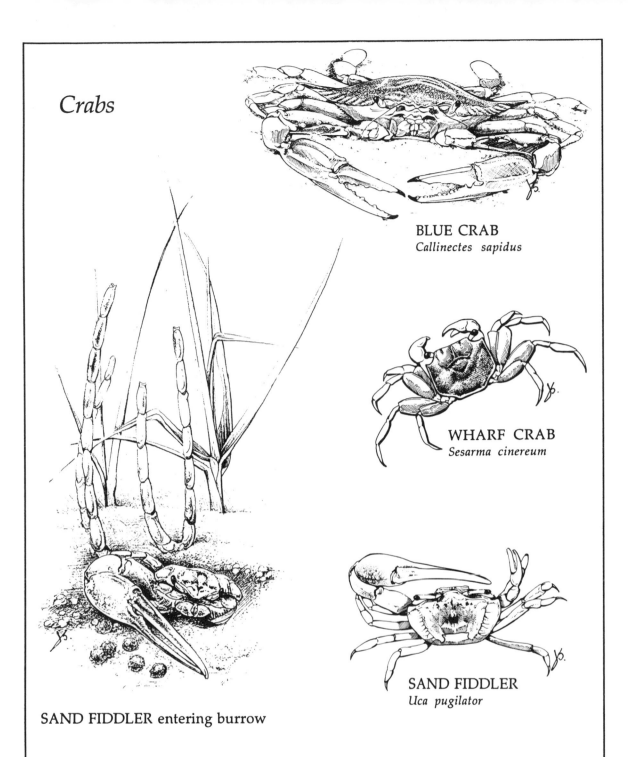

BLUE CRAB
Callinectes sapidus

WHARF CRAB
Sesarma cinereum

SAND FIDDLER
Uca pugilator

SAND FIDDLER entering burrow

BLUE CRAB: large aquatic crab that abounds in marsh creeks and sounds, green to brown shell, blue on claws, edible (shallow waters off beaches).
WHARF CRAB: 1/2-inch flat square-backed brown crab, delicate features, often found among tidal wrack and plants at the high marsh zone.
MARSH CRAB (Sesarma reticulatum): (not shown) similar to wharf crab but 1-to 2-inch in size, stout black to purple body, seen in lower intertidal marsh.
FIDDLER CRABS (Uca sp.)
  SAND FIDDLER (U. pugilator): purple on back, white claw.
  MUD FIDDLER (U. pugnax): brown body, blue line above eyes, yellow claw.
  BRACKISH-WATER FIDDLER (U. minax): larger than the other fiddlers, black back paler toward face, red dots on claw joints, white claw.

Plankton

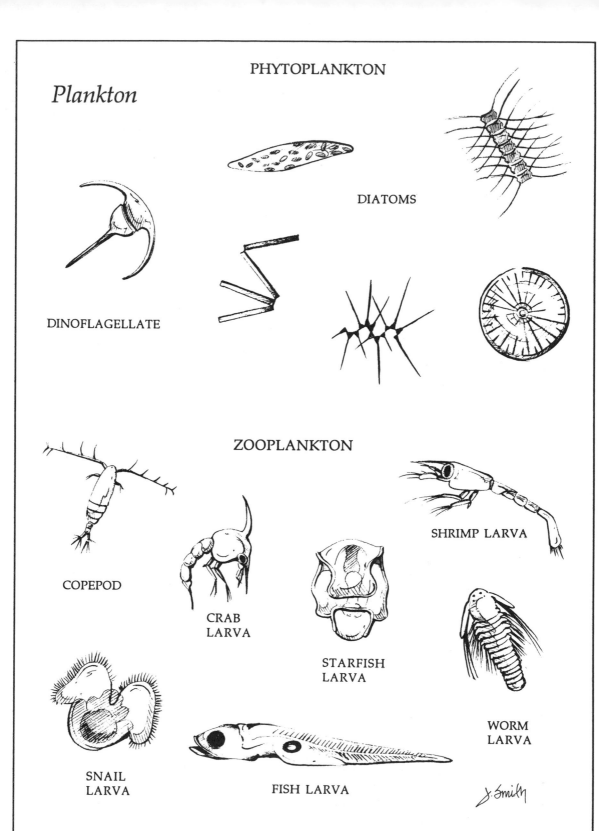

PHYTOPLANKTON

DIATOMS

DINOFLAGELLATE

ZOOPLANKTON

SHRIMP LARVA

COPEPOD

CRAB LARVA

STARFISH LARVA

WORM LARVA

SNAIL LARVA

FISH LARVA

J. Smith

PHYTOPLANKTON: Diatoms and dinoflagellates are microscopic algae and are a major producer for the animals of the salt marsh and ocean. ZOOPLANKTON: The microscopic copepods and the larval stages of many of the animals of the salt marsh are the major consumers of phytoplankton and smaller zooplankton. These provide a vital food source for the animals growing in these nursery grounds.

Reading List

Books

1. *Life and Death of a Salt Marsh*, John and Mildred Teal, Ballantine Books.

2. *Seasons of the Salt Marsh*, David Allen Gates, Chatham Press.

3. *Portrait of an Island*, John and Mildred Teal, Univ. of Georgia Press.

4. *Sea Islands of Georgia*, Count D. Gibson, Univ. of Georgia Press.

5. *Tideland Treasures*, Todd Ballantine, Deerfield Publishing, Inc.

6. *The Edge of the Sea*, Rachel Carson, Houghton Mifflin, Co.

7. *Living with the Georgia Shore*, Tonya D. Clayton et al, Duke Univ. Press.

8. *Beaches Are Moving*, W. Kaufman and Orrin Pilkey, Anchor Press.

9. *St. Simons Island, a summary of its history*, Edwin Green, Arner Publications. (Under new title: History and Mystery of St. Simons).

10. *Historic Glimpses of St. Simons Island*, 1736-1924, The Coastal Georgia Historical Society, St. Simons Island, Ga.

11. *Georgia's Land of the Golden Isles*, B. Vanstory, Univ. of Georgia Press.

Field Guides and Handbooks

1. *Seashore Animals of the Southeast*, Edward Ruppert and Richard Fox, Univ. of South Carolina Press.

2. *A Field Guide to the Atlantic Seashore*, Kenneth Gosner, Houghton Mifflin, Co.

3. *The Erotic Ocean*, Jack Rudloe, E.P. Dutton, Inc.

4. *A Guide to Field Identification: Seashells of North America*, Tucker Abbott, Golden Press.

5. *Beachcomber's Guide to the Golden Isles*, Fr. Bertrand Dunegan, O.S.B., Benedictine Priory, Sanannah, Ga.

6. *1001 Questions Answered About the Seashore*, N. Berrill and J. Berrill, Dover Publications, Inc.

7. *Wildflowers of the Southeastern United States*, Wilber Duncan and Leonard Foote, Univ. of Georgia Press.

8. *Seaside Plants of the Gulf and Atlantic Coasts*, Wilber and Marion Duncan, Smithsonian Institution Press.

9. *Trees of the Southeastern United States*, Wilber and Marion Duncan, Wormsloe Foundation Publications.

10. *Native Flora of the Golden Isles*, Gladys Fendig and Esther Stewart, Produced in St. Simons Island, Ga.

11. *A Guide to the Georgia Coast*, Georgia Conservancy. Printed by Miller Press, Jacksonville, FL.

12. *A Field Guide to the Birds*, Roger Peterson, Houghton Mifflin Co.

13. *Birds of North America*, Chandler Robbins et al, Golden Press.

14. *A Field Guide to Jekyll Island*, Taylor Schoettle, Univ. of Georgia Printing Dept.

15. *A Field Guide to Sea Island*, Taylor Schoettle, Univ. of Georgia Printing Dept.

APPENDIX D
Bibliography

1. Fox, W. T. 1983. *At the Sea's Edge.* Prentice Hall Press, New York, N.Y., p. 43.

2. Richards, H. G. 1968. "Illustrated fossils of the Georgia coastal plain." Reprinted by the Georgia Dept. of Mines, Mining and Geology from Richards' articles in the Georgia Mineral Newsletter, Academy of Natural Sciences, Philadelphia, Pa.

3. Hoyt, J. H. 1968. "Geology of the Golden Isles and Lower Georgia Coastal Plain," Conference on the Future of the Marshlands and Islands of Georgia, p. 26.

4. Titus, J. G. 1988. "Sea level rise and wetland loss: an overview." Office of Policy Analysis, United States Environmental Protection Agency, Government Printing Office, Washington, D.C.

5. Kaufmann, W. and O. H. Pilkey. 1979. *Beaches Are Moving.* Anchor Press, Doubleday, N.Y.

6. Schoettle, H. E. T. 1987. *Field Guide to Jekyll Island.* University of Georgia Printing Dept., 2ed, Sea Grant College Program, Athens, Ga.

7. Schoettle, H. E. T. 1985. *Field Guide to Sea Island.* University of Georgia Printing Dept., Sea Island Company, Sea Island, Ga.

8. Green, R. E. 1989. *St. Simons Island: A Brief Summary of Its History.* Arner Publications, Rome, N.Y.

9. Cate, M. D. 1963. "Gascoigne Bluff." Reprinted from "American Neptune," Vol. 23, No. 2 by Ft. Frederica Association, St. Simons Island, Ga. p. 14.

10. McKay, F. P. 1978. *More Fun than Heaven.* Valkyrie Press, Inc.,St. Petersburg, Fl.

11. Griffin, M. M. and V. J. Henry 1984. "Historical changes in the mean high water shoreline of Georgia." Bulletin 98. Georgia Department of Natural Resources, Georgia Geologic Survey, Atlanta, Ga. p. 64-66.

12. Olson Associates, Inc. "Feasibility Study of Glynn County, Georgia Beach Restoration." Executive Report, 1988. p. 22.

13. National Research Council 1990. *Decline of the Sea Turtles: Causes and Prevention.* National Academy Press, Washington D.C.

14. Gould, J. 1991. A descendent and resident whose family residence dates back to colonial days. Personal Communication.

15. Stevens, E. L. 1931. "How Old Are the Live Oaks?" Am. Forests,Vol. 37.

16. Coder, K. D. 1989. "Live Oak, State Tree of Georgia." University of Georgia Cooperative Extension Service Publication. #309.

17. Coggins, J. 1969. *Ships and Seamen of the American Revolution.* Stackpole Books, Harrisburg, Pa.

18. Wood, V. S. 1981. *Live Oaking: Southern Timber for Tall Ships.* Northeastern Univ. Press, Boston, Ma.

19. "Columbus and the Land of Ayllón." Sept., 1993, Seminar, Darien, Ga.

About the Author

Taylor feeding a pileated woodpecker. one of the many birds he has nurtured back to the wild.

Taylor Schoettle was born in Philadelphia. After receiving BS and MS degrees in physiology and zoology, he taught high school biology for 12 years. Over those years he amassed a fine collection of snakes and birds with which he gave lectures in the Philadelphia area, and which eventually led to a zoo career. Taylor curated three zoos: in Puerto Rico, Oklahoma City and El Paso. In El Paso Taylor was greatly moved by the scenes of the movie "Conrack," a great part of which was filmed on St. Simons (see Site 15). This impression was instrumental in the Schoettle family eventually moving to St. Simons Island.

In 1979 Taylor became a Marine Education Specialist with the University of Georgia Marine Extension Service in Brunswick. For the next two years while offering a wide range of marine and coastal education programs, he became aware that his programs were not nearly enough to meet the range and quantity of the interest groups. Out of this spawned the writing of three field guides and the other publications listed on the facing page.

In 1982, a docent program was conceived by Taylor to help meet the needs of the residents and visitors to the coast. To date the docents have reached over 100,000 people with a variety of regularly scheduled nature walks and boat rides on Jekyll, St. Simons and Sea Islands. They also conduct classes, and walks for Elderhostels and academic groups of all ages.

To meet the increasing demand of school groups from Georgia and neighboring states, Taylor conceived, with the University of Georgia 4-H Program, the Jekyll Island Environmental Education Center, which today houses and instructs over 20,000 students and teachers each year. Later, he assisted in the development of two other centers at Tybee Island, Savannah and at Honey Creek, Dover Bluff.

Now independent, Taylor conducts lecture and field programs for a wide variety of groups. He trains interpreting staff at the various environmental centers, and maintains his work with the docents. Between appointments, Taylor continues to produce publications on coastal topics, and compose songs about the coast, environmental ethics, and God. He sails and fishes whenever he can.

List of Publications:

A Field Guide to Jekyll Island. Georgia Sea Grant College Program, University of Georgia, Athens, Ga.

A Field Guide to Sea Island. Georgia Sea Grant College Program and The Sea Island Co., Sea Island, Ga.

A Naturalist's Guide to St. Simons Island. Watermarks Printing, St. Simons Island, Ga.

"The Blue Crab" (videotape). Georgia Sea Grant College Program, University of Georgia Marine Extension Service, Brunswick, Ga.

A Study Approach to the Georgia Coast: Unit I, The Ocean Beach; Unit 2, A Profile of a Salt Marsh; Unit 3, Organisms of the Dock, Georgia Sea Grant Program, University of Georgia, Athens, Ga. Units are individually available.

Lady St. Simons, you sit by the sea
Veiled in your gray-green, live oak canopy.
A queen among beauties which close to you surround,
The sandy barrier islands of Georgia abound.

Taylor Schoettle